WOMAN:
a collaboration of thoughts and feelings.

Alexandra Freeman
@mamalovesto_write

To my daughter, I hope these tales of womanhood
bring you solace as you grow.

Acknowledgements

Thank you to all the inspirational women who contributed to this project of love.

Alex Morrison - @alexmorrison27
Alicia Maynard - @lissymay
Allegra Harrison - bodhitwinkle@icloud.com
Amy Oldland
Anna Day - @annadaytweets
Annoushka Reger - @annnnoushka
Beth Smith
Charlotte Wye
Collette Nurse
Elelia Ferro - Facebook page: Married to the Marshes
Elle Pearson - @ellepearson
Gemma Wright - @gem_wright_
Hannah Rose
Holly Von-Broen
Imogen Nurse
Janet R Smith - janet.smith850@gmail.com
Josie Williams
Laura Mathias
Lily Hopkins - @themeffsuk
Lorna Freeman
Lorna Reeve
Lorna Stuart-Hunt - @_nbdlsh
Mary C. Reilly - maryccreilly@gmail.com
Natasha Ramsey - @gorgusdoc
Nyambura Nyganda - @NyamburaNyganda
Pat Taylor - @chasingrainbows6
Paula Johnston - @paulajohnstonauthor
Paula Stafford
Penny Benedetti - penny25@live.co.uk
Rebbecca O'Dell
Rebbecca Allenby - @rebecca.and.her.boys
Rio Carciero - @riocarciero
Rowena Macalay - @chezwink
Roxanne Rodrigues-Betts - @copyrox_ and @rocksea_rocksand
Sara Awiesha - @sara_awiesha

Sara Hawkins - @sazzlehawkins and @average_girl_runs
Sarah Freeman
Sarah Hayden-Woods - www.haydenwoodscreative.com
Stephanie Mantle - @beautifullybookishbysteph
Susan Anne Harvey - harveysue9@gmail.com
Tina Catchpole - bodhitwinkle@icloud.com
Yolanda Russell - @_yolandarussell

Special thanks

Proofreader and word wizard - Di Bignell

Rock Legend - Suzi Quatro
Insta: @suziquatroreal
Twitter: @Suzi_Quatro
Facebook.com/Suziquatrorocks
www.suziquatro.com

Introduction to book

This book is a selection of short stories from women from all different backgrounds. An intimate collection of personal stories looking at various aspects of 'womanhood'.
Some pieces are written by established writers and some by women who have never written before…

Preface in Poetry from the Author

We are doting mothers, dutiful wives, enduring saints and
luminous figures of beauty,
We've been told how to love and what to wear and that beauty
is only skin deep,
That there IS perfect.
But we are more, so much more.
We define beauty in strength and in unity,
Each shape and race and curvature stunning in all its glory.
We birthed life into homes, cradling crying infants into dusk
and dawn,
Enduring unearthly pain in synchronised harmony.
The rhythm of pain escaping and making all that surrounds us.
We were a movement ensuring every voice was heard,
A voice so often stifled but still we will not stay quiet,
We will shout words of resistance and live openly painting the
streets with true equality,
Healing from purple bruises and splintered bones we stand
and fight again,
A new strength that fills rooms and captures hearts.

Being alone is okay

Nothing quite prepares you to be alone, from life skills lessons in school to watching films about go-getting women who must have it all, to hearing first-hand accounts from friends and family; none of that even comes close to matching up to actually living through it.

From the outside with the naivety of youth, growing up and relying on yourself seems like it's going to be easy, the next natural step in life.

Obviously, follow the plan you have set out for yourself whilst your body and mind were still forming in youth or adolescence – finish education, leave family home, work, pair off with someone (ideally whilst you're still, or at least close to being, a teenager – really minimise that time spent on your own), create your own version of a family, die hand in hand with your lover in old age like that scene in the Notebook – simple really, a walk in the park.

Nearly everyone I grew up with had their plans for life pretty much set out like that; parts obviously were interchangeable such as when you finished education, the work you did, what kind of partner or even partners you wanted, how you saw your family dynamic - whether it was dogs or babies or a lizard with a surprising amount of love to give - but the core steps remained the same; after all, why would you ever plan for any kind of alternative life to that? A life plan that doesn't involve at least one other in it seems unheard of. From an early age it is drilled into us that being alone is the worst possible path we could encounter.

Films and television programmes show us person after person who's struggling through life on their own, hapless and bumbling, only to be saved at the end by someone coming in, sweeping them off their feet and saving them from a life on their own.

Or these shows perpetuate that people on their own are unlovable and devoid of the ability to love, grouchy insufferable humans, with being alone to be something that should be feared - a warning to the viewer to not end up this way. Not one person ever came to my school to give a talk on solitude, I remember very few films about someone being alone and being happy, no one ever said that a life alone was just as much of a valid and okay life as one spent with others.

I was twenty-one when I was thrust into the world of being independent and self-reliant; my change in lifestyle came with much more of a crash and a bang than the gentle waltz that I had expected to come. I would describe myself as growing up headstrong, I was a determined child who knew what she wanted, but I was also flighty with a knack for not applying myself when needed but most things still working out in my favour. I never expected life not to turn out the way I first imagined because why would I?

Up till this point in my life I had just taken every obstacle in my stride. Challenges were exactly that: a test of my patience but nothing more. However, at the beginning of 2014, in the space of just three months, my life irreversibly changed. My housemate had moved out with little to no notice, my family refused to let me move back with them, I had suffered an awful sexual assault, and I moved into a flat on my own – none of this fit into the map of life that I had made for myself. I was left shocked at the harsh realities of life and felt, without want for a better word, alone.

When I first moved into my flat, I had no working television, I had no internet installed, and in all honesty, I had never spent that much time on my own. I had moved from a busy family home into a house share with my friends that was affectionately referred to as a shelter for all the waifs and strays, with people constantly revolving through its doors, to it being just me.

I was terrified of my own thoughts at that time, terrified of silence, terrified of being on my own. Every evening after work I invited friends over to come fill the void; failing that, I watched endless repeats of the same DVDs over and over again. I played music from my phone of songs that held happy memories or, more often than not, I went out drinking to placate the desperate need to not be left with myself. I can't pretend that it was an easy transition in life and, even if I was filling my time as much as possible with others and external stimulation, I still felt very much alone.

However, at some point within that first year something changed. I left it longer between the repeats of DVDs, music didn't need to be constantly playing, I didn't go out as often, and I stopped feeling the need to have people over all the time. I did, and still do, have a fantastic group of friends around me that brought light to the darkest moments, but you can't depend on other people to always be there when you need it; that isn't realistic or fair on either them or you. At some point you need to be that friend for yourself. Gradually, with no momentous change in day-to-day life, I became less terrified of the silence; in fact, I grew to love it.

I realised that I was no longer terrified of myself or my own thoughts and started to treat myself in the ways I would treat someone else, with kindness and compassion. I started to listen to what I really needed and required, with even my darkest thoughts needing to be heard and addressed.

I became softer towards myself and made a conscious effort to stop talking to myself negatively. I began to actively seek out my own passions, be aware of what made me happy, take up new hobbies, enjoy my own company and the person I was becoming over time. I made, and still make, myself smile and laugh on a daily basis. Over time I began to realise that being alone was not the terrifying prospect I had been sold my whole life. I was no less worthy of love, nor had my ability to be loving diminished as a result of being on my own, if anything I was now experiencing self-love for the first time on a large scale.

I became aware, regardless of plans I may have once set myself, that I was everything that I had ever needed or would need in life. Life on my own wasn't this scary void of nothingness, it wasn't that bad or even bad at all to be on my own.

I have no idea what life holds for me anymore; in many ways, I have stopped making any real long-term plans. Life feels too full of variants to abide by a checklist of events that I might wish to happen, and I am okay with that. I have no idea whether my future is to be spent with others or alone and frankly either is fine. I know that I made it through points that I didn't think I would, that I found a friend in myself and that I let go of a fear that was put on me by others and expectations. Stripping away my preconceived ideas about being alone has allowed me to build the best possible life for myself. Everything within my life is a welcome addition and not because I am missing anything. Once I had come to this realisation I felt truly liberated.

I have built my life to what I want it to be, I am happy, in a place I love living. The shows I watch and the music I listen to are because I want to and not as some kind of self-medication for silence. The people I have in my life and surround myself with are there because I want them to be, not because I need them to fill any emptiness within myself.

I still feel alone but that is okay. I am alone and I am also everything I need. I am no longer lonely.

Alicia, 28

Who am I?

White
Anglian
Decent from aristocracy
Drowning in privilege
Surrounded by hypocrisy
Sit up
Stand straight
No elbows on the table
Pronunciate
Stand tall

Am I my mother?
Bending to fit
Searching for approval
Giving my self
My body
My soul
My all

Am I my father?
Resisting the establishment
Rebelling against all
Yearning to be different
To be special
To stand for something
Anything
Never to fall

Am I the boy I first kissed?
That kissed me
The one who caressed me
Friends cheering on
Not knowing what to do with my tongue

Am I my body?
My breasts
My ovaries
My skin
The chicken pox scar on my face

An ear
A leg
Don't scratch
Don't touch
It will never go

Am I the ones who have touched it?
Tormented it
Used it
Abused it
Loved it
Scrutinised it
Longed for it
Shamed it

Am I my weight?
The digits on the scale
Haunting me
Taunting me
All that I have indulged
Forced to evacuate
Don't take up space
It's not safe

Am I my bones?
Brittle and broken
Weak
Bent out of shape
Not long enough
Not strong enough
Not tall

Am I my eyes?
All that they have seen
The tears that have fallen
The lines that surround them
Hidden by toxins
But still there
Impending
Underneath it all

Am I my age?
My impending demise
The number of years I have lived
That I have withstood
That I have concealed
Hidden and pumped
Filled and disguised

Am I the youth?
I am failing to cling to
To claw back
The times I long to revisit
The times I yearn to forget
To reset
To redo
That I regret

Am I the touches?
The strokes
The pain I have caused
The pain I have endured
The hurt imposed
The scars inflicted
Paraded
Invaded
Exposed

Am I the darkness that has devoured?
That has absorbed
Embraced
That has led
That has seduced
That has held me
Betrayed me

Am I the children I have birthed?
That grew inside
Stretched my skin
Pushed my organs
Made space for their own
And the ones I did not

Am I their successes?
Their pain
Their fear
Their joy
Their anger
Their love
Their loss

Am I the music I consume?
Move to
Scream with
Cry for
The sound that flows through
That rips me apart
And makes me whole

Am I the words I have read?
That I have written
That I have said
That have empowered
That have moulded
Words I regret
Echoing through my mind
And the words not said

Am I all?
Am I none?
Will I ever know?

Charlotte, 33

Sarah's story - Part 1

It is a truism that the lives of women in previous centuries are largely undocumented and especially true of those of working-class women, so I am fortunate to have discovered so much about my great grandmother Sarah. I had always known that she had been committed to the Durham County Lunatic Asylum but virtually everything else I believed, passed on my grandfather Tom, the second of her five sons turns out to be family myth, possibly told to console a heartbroken and bewildered child.

Sarah, born in 1847, was the only daughter in a family which included two half - brothers from her father's first marriage and a younger brother. Originally agricultural labourers from Cumberland, the family had moved into County Durham and mining.

Sarah married my great grandfather Robson when she was 18 and seven months pregnant in 1866 and her daughter, Elizabeth, was born seven weeks later. George, their first son, was born in 1868. Robson was, in family legend, an agitator for better conditions for working miners and therefore blacklisted by coal owners. He was indeed fined six shillings- a tidy sum in those days, about a third of the average weekly pay- for wilfully damaging machinery just prior to his departure for the United States in 1869. With him were Sarah and their two children, all travelling steerage, and arriving in New York City on April 1st, 1869. From there, they went to Liberty Township, in Trumbull County, Ohio where coal had recently been discovered on Alexander McCleary's farm and to which miners from all over the world travelled in the hope of a better life but in truth from one exploitative system to another. While there, Sarah was admitted to Weston Asylum, West Virginia for 8 months. After her release she gave birth to Sarah in 1873.

How the family journeyed from New York to Ohio or how Sarah went from Liberty Township to the Weston Asylum, in West Virginia, both distances of more than 300 miles- or indeed how they managed to get back to County Durham- remains unknown.

The family then returned to County Durham and six more children were born. The 1881 census records the family as living in Normanton, Yorkshire, with Ruth, named after Sarah's mother, in the home of her uncle in Durham. Ruth died two years later, the only one of Sarah's children to die in childhood. The remaining eight lived on, married and had families of their own. Sarah's youngest child Mabel was born in November 1876. Three months later Sarah's mother died leaving Sarah bereft of her immediate family. On February 16th, 1888, Sarah was admitted to the Durham County Lunatic Asylum where she died, thirty-eight years later.

The records make grim reading. She was certified on February 15th.1888 by Robert Muir Gilchrist Binnie MD on two counts:

1. Rambling in her talk, first from one subject to another and mixing people up together, other days dull and listless, sitting gazing at the fire, without speech of any kind, abusing a neighbour one day as cause of all her trouble and saying the next day that she was the only friend she had.

2. Her sister-in-law states that on the evening of January 28th. she walked up Durham Street with nothing on but her nightdress. On several occasions she had made an attempt to set fire to house: attempted violence to her daughter with poker.

This is preceded by reference to her previous "attack" in 1871 and the information that the duration of this present "attack" is three months, that the cause is not known, that she is neither epileptic nor suicidal but is dangerous to others.

Sarah does not appear to have had anyone speaking on her behalf, neither then nor at any point in the following thirty eight years. The records are a curious mixture of what purport to be clinical observations and judgemental assessments of her character, appearance and personality. They are mostly unsigned and the status of the author never defined.

They are sometimes contradictory: one observer speaks pejoratively of her delusions. You can almost hear the outrage in "she imagines I am her son" while another reports that she " has no fixed delusions of mind". When, shortly after her admission, she is recorded as having a temperature of 102, she is prescribed doses of quinine but there is no suggestion that this might be affecting her behaviour. When at the beginning of July she is "advised" of her husband's death on June 18th of pneumonia, she takes it "quietly not seeming to realise the fact. On her son's visit she cried a great deal and insisted on being let out."

The majority of the entries, evidently from a ledger, are perfunctory and of the "No change " variety and terse to the point of indifference.In November 1891 she is transferred to the Fisherton House Asylum in Salisbury at the other end of the country. No explanation for this decision is recorded but the two previous entries on June 4th and August 16th. read: No improvement. Dull, idle, restless and mildly depressed. Fat and idle. Bothers to go home but makes no effort. Dementia advancing. These are signed. Perhaps 'A. Birt' had a good reason for the decision to transfer her or perhaps not.

She returns to the Durham County Lunatic Asylum on June 28th.1895. Although scant, the Fisherton entries from June 1893 onwards describe her as "Quiet, tractable, industrious, quiet, busy, a good ward worker but on occasions, troublesome." These entries are signed and it is clear that one recorder has difficulties that others do not.

In the years that follow, she seems to have been transferred between different sections of the Durham Asylum and there are gaps in the record. She is described in one entry as a periodic case and there are entries where there is speculation as to whether she is building up to another attack and as the years progress "No change" "Nothing to report" become the standard entry. There is never any mention of any treatment except for an incident where she fell and injured her arm, even in the last months of her life, when she was dying unpleasantly of diabetes.

I have been advised by a family member who has clinical experience in this field, that to speculate at this distance as to the nature or possible cause of Sarah's mental health problems is unprofitable and that to expect any asylum to offer more than containment, given the knowledge and practice of the times, is unreasonable and to an extent I can accept this. Nevertheless, it bothers me that Sarah was deprived of her liberty, her family- even her name.

Census records from the Durham County Lunatic Asylum give initials only and information is confined to "Inmate" and "Lunatic." While I have evidence from family letters that my grandfather made some financial contribution to her maintenance via a named doctor I have found no evidence of either in the records: her name was never mentioned in a family that never hid her having been certified. Whilst my grandfather gave Robson as one of his eldest son's names, none of his four daughters had Sarah.

Sarah died only eight years before I was born. My mother knew less about her than I do now and according to her my grandmother had seen Sarah only once. The story, believed and handed on by my grandfather, was that his mother had been left by his father, who had gone off to America to seek his fortune and never heard of again.

The story that his mother, desperate in poverty and distress, had made dresses for the girls and when she completed these had thrown them on the fire and for this reason was certified, turns out to be untrue. Perhaps this was a story he was told by well-meaning relatives trying to soften the blow of separation and the dispersal of his family. When I was lamenting to my grandfather, then well into his eighties, my inability to get my son to give up sucking his thumb, he smiled sadly and said "I still do that before I go to sleep" and I saw, even then, though I knew nothing about Sarah, not the formidable man I knew but a boy missing his Mam.

Beth, 86

Gorjus Doc

Of all the names people call me, Dr. Ramsey, Dr. Tasha, Natasha, and Tasha, Gorjus Doc- which is my business name and Insta handle - is by far my favorite. People always want to know, what does Gorjus Doc even mean? And it's not really a simple answer, because it dates all the way back to when I was a teen.

There are two assumptions people usually make about me from the name Gorjus Doc. I prefer a more urban/ "ghetto" vernacular. Because of course, Gorjus is just a play on the word gorgeous. And the second is I think very highly of myself, because by definition the word gorgeous means showily brilliant or magnificent. While these assumptions are somewhat accurate there is so much more to the nickname. It dates all the way back to my converse, flat twists, and gel pens days in middle school.

Flash back to 2003, back when everyone's favorite shows were 106 and Park on BET and TRL on MTV with all the new songs and latest trends. Back when you still had to pay for text messaging, SideKick phones were all the rage, and you called your friends on the house phone. Back when you weren't cool unless you had Nike Air Forces, Rocawear jackets, and Pepe jeans. Given my parents were struggling immigrants from Jamaica and we had no money, I by default was pretty lukewarm. My mom loved shopping at the discount stores, where she could buy our clothes, lace curtains and table runners, and school supplies all in one. So that meant I had NO name brand clothes. And I got one pair of shoes per school year, so that meant every Saturday I had to line up all my sneakers and get to work cleaning them with a toothbrush and a rag.

Although I wasn't the best dressed or most fashionable person in my grade, I had a few things going for me: I was smart and I could draw so I used that to my advantage to make friends. The cool kids took me under their wing, and as long as I gave them the answers to the math homework in the bathroom before homeroom, we were good.

This was also the era when everyone gave themselves nicknames: Princess, Dime Piece, Shorty, Cutie all spelled incorrectly and in bubbly letters with different patterns and colors. If your parents had enough money, you might even get your nickname customized on a double plated nameplate necklace or name plate belt. I used my art skills to master drawing bubble letters and when we had a free period at school, I would sketch all these creative names on the chalkboard.

So by default, I had to come up with my own name, one that was worthy of making its way to the chalkboard or on a nameplate necklace. I thought of the word gorgeous, and felt that it was suitable because it not only meant beautiful, but also elegant, magical, and valuable like a diamond. Thus the name Gorjus was born and I was sure to draw a little diamond on top to dot the J. Even though I would never be able to afford cool jewelry or a belt with my name on it, I made sure to doodle it all over my notebooks and tattoo it all over my skin with gel pen and markers.

Despite the nickname I gave myself, and the countless notebooks I scribbled in, I didn't feel "Gorjus". I had kinky hair, chocolate skin, and buck teeth with a gap and I grew breasts and hips before I know what to do with them. It took random cars beeping the horn at me as I skipped to the bodega to realize I had grown women body parts. I always wished I could be petite and slim like my friends, or have long silky curly hair and fair skin like my Hispanic friends, or light color eyes like my mixed friends. The world told me I wasn't beautiful, that I wasn't Gorjus.

My parents tried to counter the negative messages I was receiving all around me. We had pictures of prominent black leaders all throughout our house, and they both identified as Rastafarians, with long thick curly manes that directly countered the European beauty standards I had been seeing on TV. And their outward Jamaican-ness was ripe for material for getting picked on for being one of few Caribbean Americans in my school.

22

And it certainly didn't help that my mom would roll up to the playground to pick me up after school blasting reggae tunes with a Jamaican flag hanging from the rear view mirror. At that time in my life, I felt like an alien from another planet, and I just wanted to fit in. I wanted to look like the glamorous video models in the music videos and magazines.

It took me a long time to embrace my culture, the skin I was in, the hair growing on my head, and the gap I still have to this day. It took me a long time to actually feel like the Gorjus I had doodled all over my notebooks. I had to fake it till I made it. I had to reprogram the way I think and the things I watched, the things I believed and challenge what I was taught by the media and people around me.

I had to look in the mirror every morning and remind myself of the words my parents would say to me: that black was beautiful, that I was beautiful, that I came from strength and resilience, and that I was loved wholly- from the tips of my toes to the depths of my soul. I stopped hiding from the sun, and let the sun rays kiss my skin. I stopped perming my hair and let the coils hang free. I stopped focusing on the outside and nurtured who I was on the inside to discover what it really meant to be Gorjus.

Like a diamond, I'm complex. I'm strong, yet fragile. I am transparent, yet full of twists and turns like the lattices that create a diamond. I continue to transform into something polished and beautiful with pressure and time. And I know my value and my worth. With time I have become Gorjus, and once I became a doctor, the Doc part followed.

Natasha, 31

<u>Finally Free</u>

After being asked to write a submission for this book I changed my mind about what to write and how to write it a hundred times. I wanted to write about a relationship that has deeply impacted my life but the fear of being judged for 'putting up with it' has previously prevented me from sharing this story. I guess that's an abusive relationship -based on control and conversion – and still in some ways controlling me to this day.

I left my first marriage at the young age of 24. On the outside, we seemed to have it all: a beautiful child, a home together and good jobs, but the truth was we had met young and unfortunately drifted apart, finishing things in messy circumstances. I decided to leave our home in Edinburgh with my three-year-old daughter to move back to my hometown of Colchester where I hoped I could restart my life with the support of my family. It wasn't quite the new beginning I had in mind and on returning home I was greeted by a mother in the grips of an ongoing cycle of alcohol dependency and a new and abusive partner. Looking back on things, abusive relationships were all I had known growing up and perhaps this had something to do with the pattern of relationships I had found myself in.

After deciding it was best not to stay with my Mother I sought refuge in a hostel. I was relieved to have a roof over my head but I'd be lying if I said it wasn't a shock going from our beautiful family home to an apartment stained in blood, and that could only be described as vile. The building was full of people suffering with addiction, the very aliment I had gone there to leave behind, and I couldn't escape the feeling of unsafety. I put my daughter to sleep every night in my cupboard. Why? Because every night I fell asleep to the noise and screams outside and I feared my door would come crashing down.

A few months later we went to stay in Edinburgh with some friends, a welcome sense of normality for my daughter when I got a phone call to tell me they had found a flat. At the time my Mum was in a period of sobriety and for the first time things where looking up.

After an initial glee filled period after moving in together, my mood came crashing down. I felt scared and alone, away from my friends in Edinburgh and unsure what do next. After sending my daughter off to school, I would sleep my days away. I fell into a pit of despair and found myself using online dating for company. This is where I met him. We will call him 'Jack' as to this day as deep down I'm still scared. After an introduction from a friend I found myself welcoming the man who would change my life forever into my home.

The first time we met I was instantly attracted. I found his manly presence comforting. He was smooth, charming and he spent the night telling me all about himself, including his violent past.This should have been a huge red flag, but after explaining he was misunderstood I couldn't help but find his seeming transparency admirable. He put emphasis on his loyalty which instantly drew me to him as loyalty wasn't something I had experienced much of my life and was something I wanted more than anything. I can now look back and see the signs of narcissism and sociopathic tendencies were there from the beginning but this wasn't so obvious at the time.

He maintained from the start he only wanted friendship and thus began a cycle of him using me for comfort and sex. I quickly found myself deeply emotionally invested and it is clear to me now the power balance was off from the start. He knew I would never refuse him, that I would never say no. He had entered my life at the perfect time when I was most vulnerable and needing someone the most - no matter how bad for me that person was.

I soon found myself in a cycle of providing for him and I would regularly cook. He would visit and this is when the first incident of abuse that really stands out happened. I was bent over cooking and he stood over me with a presence. He told me I looked different. 'What do you mean? 'I replied and with that he took his hand and pushed them down my knickers. I stood there in shock and panic as I realised he was checking to see if I had slept with another man. Panic and fear took over as I laughed nervously.

'Are you joking?'

That's when he hit me in the throat. I just stood there. Full of fear, pain and confusion as I just continued to cook.

Despite this incident and several others, I made the regrettable decision to allow Jack to move in with me. Things of course only got worse.

Jack would hit me, emotionally and physically abuse me, and use the house to have friends over and take cocaine at his leisure with no consideration for me or my daughter. The abuse escalated, further and further until violence was no longer a secret between us. One night we were sat in our living room, music and drinks flowing between the group. We sat on one sofa together, his friend adjacent, and that's when he punched me out of nowhere. He punched me so hard blood spilled from my mouth as I begged for an explanation.

"Because you're a c**t he said.

I had never felt so powerless. I hid away in my daughter's room as it was unlikely he would come in there and that was where I felt safest. Unfortunately, this was far from the last incident of violence. It wasn't just the physical assault that slowly chipped away at any fraction of self-worth I had left: it was the emotional abuse. He called me ugly, disgusting and held me down telling me no-one would ever want me and I believed it. I smoked frequently in a desperate attempt to lose weight and found myself despising my body and the core of who I was.

It was when the abuse effected my daughter that my self-worth was at its lowest, as even now I fail to understand how I could allow it to happen. After his nights of drinking and binging on drugs he would scream at us from the bedroom to keep the noise down as I desperately attempted to keep my daughter quiet, and whispering at home became the new normal. He would often belittle her, and these for me are some of the most painful memories that I live with.

Jack desperately wanted a child of his own and despite my objection he would regularly force himself onto me in attempt to impregnate me which lead me to a secret doctor's trip to get a coil. I will never forget the pity in that doctor's eyes. He looked down at my bruised body with such sympathy. 'These are some of the worst bruises I've ever seen' he said with such concern and sympathy, but it was second nature for me to lie.

'I've just fallen' I would reply.

He was an animal. Now let go from the army due to violent behaviour and completely consumed in rage, he bit, hit, punched, spat on, humiliated and taunted me regularly. If I did ever decide to hide away from him, when I'd finally had enough, he would somehow find me, ripping down my door if he had to, and at this point in my life I honestly thought this would be my life forever.

After another forced entry into the flat and another blazing row, the neighbour reported him. I remember actually being quite cross at the time having to defend myself as a mother and not recognising myself as the victim I was, but this was really the turning point for me. It was after my daughter was interviewed that everything hit home; reality slapped me hard in the face and I swore never to see him again. The police, social services and women's refuge got involved and I am now eternally grateful they did. Every time he turned up he was arrested and although I lived in fear for quite some time I did manage to get away.

With the help of my extended family, support from social services and the police I was one the lucky ones. Fast forward: I am 11 years into a loving a committed marriage to a loyal loving man who treats me with the love and respect that I now realise I deserve. My dark days will forever haunt me. It has taken me a long time to forgive myself for exposing myself - and particularly my daughter - to such dangers but I now recognize I was the victim of abuse taking comfort in an abuse cycle I had always known.

Today I choose to focus on the strength it took to rebuild my life and move away from this cycle and I am grateful for having a second chance at life. Jack is now serving time in prison for the murder of his partner and this will forever be a harrowing reminder of how close I came to the same fate. For anyone who is in the grips of an abusive relationship I can honestly say there is another world waiting. One where you don't have to live in fear and torment. One where you can be free.

Anonymous

The Mermaid of Pin Mill

Where the waders peg the mud,
inside a shipwreck's whaley bones,
a mermaid quietly sunk in silt,
awaits the tide to take her home.

That night while all her sisters sleep,
so silently she swims ashore,
to watch the writer at his craft,
behind a stained-glass houseboat door.

But Francis cannot work tonight,
his hands feel too alone to write,
his torch leads to a warm pub fire,
the mermaid quickly dives from sight.

Our hero checks the coast is clear
and heaves herself onto the cliff,
the chestnut burrs spike in her scales,
the sight of blood, it scares her stiff.

Ahead a white witch wrapped in black
works her silver besom broom,
the birch sheds stars upon the ground,
lighting up the woodland gloom.

Dawn plays long low orange notes,
a moony sky calls up the sun,
the mermaid wakes to find two legs,
and all her bloody scratches are gone.

Francis on his morning walk
spots the mermaid on the moss,
she doesn't seem to know her name
and shimmers with a fishy gloss.

He picks her up inside his coat
and takes her to his Blue Bird den,
to his surprise she sits and writes -
'Can I borrow your shiny pen?'.

Deep inside the barges hull
Francis tries to pin her down.
Our mermaid thinks, oh not again,
another one I have to drown.

All men who meet a Mermaid fair,
they always think the same -
we're all sirens or submissives,
they only have themselves to blame.

She grips the writer by his hands
and quickly drags him to the shore,
he screams and splutters in the water,
she pulls him down a little more.

Francis does not want to die,
he pleads she takes his shed next door,
she grabs the keys and then the pen,
and pins, NO ENTRY to the door.

Neighbourly they quietly live,
along the river Orwell path,
occasionally they share some prose,
or a wary salt night bath.

Elelia, 43

A life in Blue

In August 1991, I walked through the gates of Hendon Training School aged 24 for the start of what would become an amazing career that was to span some 30 years and begin the roller coaster journey of becoming a female police officer.

At this time, women were still very much in a minority within the police service, where the height limit requirement had only recently been quashed, women were allowed to wear trousers for the first time and, thankfully for me, the tradition of all female officers being stamped with the station stamp on a particular part of their body was no longer practised! All my supervisors and senior officers were men and out of a team of 30 officers I was one of only two females.

Hendon was my home for the next 20 weeks where I learnt all the basics I needed to help me on my way, including public order training with police horses, learning criminal law, lifesaving, how to march, handcuffing techniques and of course wearing a uniform for the first time. Life certainly was very different behind the gates of Hendon in terms of routine and discipline. Every morning at 7.30am we would find out which classes would be 'on parade' at 8.15am for an inspection by a senior officer in full uniform.

This certainly did not give those who were still asleep a very much time to get up, dressed and 'de-fluffed' in time for the drill sergeant to call us to attention before the eagle-eyed senior officer came out to check our uniform and shoes were as clean and shiny as they should be. Those lucky enough to escape the dreaded parade would have the luxury of an extra 30 minutes to get ready and have a leisurely breakfast.

One particularly freezing cold morning we were one of the unlucky classes to be called to parade, which always took place at the front of the training school and next to the statue of Sir Robert Peel.

It wasn't long after we took our places that I heard some giggling and whispering amongst my fellow trainees, when my attention was drawn to Sir Roberts statue where I immediately noticed that somebody had decided to wrap a bright red scarf round his neck! This was quite an achievement considering the statue was about 10 to 12 foot tall! It felt like it was the longest parade ever during which we were all desperately trying to contain ourselves while the unsuspecting senior officer moved between the ranks to inspect us.

Towards the end of the parade the misdemeanour was pointed out to him by another member of staff, which as you can imagine did not go down too well. He demanded to know by the end of the day who was responsible for this so-called prank and that if the culprit did not own up then we would all be held responsible. The truth did eventually come out several days later but only after we had all been punished by doing evening patrols of the estate. Apparently, a few of the lads on their way home from the pub the previous night had dared each other to provide Sir Robert with his extra clothing!

At the conclusion of my twenty weeks training we all took part in a very formal passing out parade to mark the occasion. This was and still is one of the proudest days of my life. From almost our very first day we had started to learn the drill we would need to perform what for some was a very difficult exercise. The coordination required for marching did not come easy for all and I still chuckle to myself when I look back at some of the folk that found putting one foot in front of the other such a tricky task.

The parade included police horses, the Metropolitan Police Band and a reviewing officer who was there to inspect us and later make a speech. Leading up to the parade, we were all very excited to learn who it may be as in previous intakes they had been lucky enough to have a member of the royal family or even the Commissioner. I have to say there was a tinge of disappointment when we learnt that Roy Hattersley, the leader of the Labour Party, was to be our reviewing officer.

But despite some of the jokes about how he would perform on the day, he gave an excellent speech and made us all feel very special. The parade all went very well and I was very proud to show off my new uniform and marching skills to my family. My only regret was that my beloved father was unable to witness this very special day after he sadly and suddenly passed away three years before then. I know he would have absolutely loved seeing his little girl in uniform and be bursting with pride.

Not long after my passing out parade in January 1991 I started my very first posting as a police constable at Barking Police Station where I began my street duties training. This involved going out with a tutor constable who was there to guide us, help us to complete our paperwork correctly and make sure we didn't make unlawful arrests! Whilst I don't recall my very first day on the beat I do remember feeling for several weeks very much like the new kid at school and terrified of making a mistake. This next stage of my training, my probation was to last another 18 months and included taking part in continuation training at a nearby station in East Ham every three months.

Whilst the majority of this training was academic there was also some practical training one of which was to observe a post mortem - something which I was absolutely dreading. On the day in question there were eight of us in our group. Six male officers and one other female. All the guys were very excited about this forthcoming visit to the mortuary whilst myself and Cathy were the opposite and wondering how we were going to get through it as we had been given very clear instructions that we had to watch the post mortem in its entirety or we would not pass this section of our training.

Whilst I now know this wasn't true in those days it seemed to be common-place to sow seeds of fear or doubt to get us to go along to such a horrible event. Once we arrived at the mortuary our instructors left us with the very pleasant mortician who explained the procedure to us in detail and made it very clear that if at any time the group felt unwell or did not wish to continue watching, then they could leave the room and wait outside.

Within a very short period of time one by one the boys all gradually made their excuses and left the room leaving just myself and Cathy to watch the entire procedure from start to finish. I have to say once I had got past the fact it was a human being and someone's loved one I found it absolutely fascinating and felt very privileged to have witnesses something which very few people get to see in real life and such a vital procedure to establish the cause of death and what if any offences had been committed. I have to say the journey back to the police station was a lot quieter with some very pale faced male colleagues who were in awe of Cathy and I staying to the end.

During my service, I worked in a variety of roles including Domestic Violence, Child Sexual Abuse, and murder. All of these roles were challenging in their own way and no two days were ever the same. Whilst it was very stressful and demanding at times I feel proud to have helped so many people over the years and hopefully made a difference in their lives. I have also worked with some incredible people over the years and certainly felt part of a very big family. There is no doubt it has been a roller coaster at times and without doubt had an impact of my private life and relationships over the years.

So, fast forward to December 2020 when after 30 years I decided it was time to hang up my boots! I have to say it was a lot harder than I expected and whilst I felt a huge weight lift from my shoulders I did not realise how institutionalised I had become over the years and worried for a while if I had in fact done the right thing. But having gone into yet another Covid 19 lockdown I am enjoying my new-found freedom and keeping busy with lots of voluntary work until we are finally allowed back out of our homes again. In those three decades, I witnessed so many changes in law, procedures, staffing and protocol. Some for the better but sadly some not so.

In terms of how women have progressed within what was a very male dominated occupation I am pleased and proud to say that we now have our very first female Commissioner in The Met, which is wonderful. So many more women are now in senior positions within the service and opportunities for women continue to become more common place. Would I do it all over again given the choice? Most definitely. It has made me the person I am today and given me the most amazing insight into human behaviour both good and bad. It truly was the career of a lifetime.

Paula, 53

"I Don't Have to Have Kids"

I remember those words passing my 30-year-old lips. I know they were going to crush a piece of my Mother that day. I was taking away her only chance to be a grandmother as her only child. Whenever we talked about me having kids, I shared my hesitancy or lack of desire. She always told me, "you have to have at least one." And that particular day, those words, "I don't have to have kids," were an awakening of my journey in choosing. Choosing to create a life against what society had deemed to be the norm. A life that many wouldn't understand.

I had a deep knowing that I wasn't destined to be a Mom in a 'normal,' way—even as a young child. I was about eight years old when I learned what adoption was. I envisioned a home with faces of children who weren't my own. It was exciting to dream about and I was especially drawn to adoption because it seemed so 'taboo.' My young mind, consumed with thoughts like:

Why weren't adults giving children in need an opportunity to be included in a family that loved them enough to embrace them as their own?

Why weren't more adults saving those children?

Why did I need to have my own children when there were children around the world that needed love, care, and shelter?

Being raised in a single-parent home only added to my confusion. My Mom didn't date much. Her focus was on getting me through school and off to college without getting pregnant. Determined that I would not be a statistic - a young, black teen mom.

I didn't have an example of what love, marriage, and parenting looked like between two adults growing up.

I was left to figure out what relationships meant or should look like. Truth be told, I'm still confused. When puberty finally hit, I was underdeveloped in comparison to other girls my age. This meant that many of my 'firsts,' like a first kiss or first boyfriend, came later in life.

Other teen girls were dreaming of their weddings and having babies. I was figuring out how to thrive in a world when I felt so different in my desires. My dream became learning how to accept, love, and embrace the desires I had, even when they weren't the 'norm.' I had a few serious boyfriends in my twenties. I often ignored the red flags as I focused on how long it would last. I was convinced that a lasting relationship would change my mind about having children.

At 27, I was in a relationship that seemed promising. We moved in together, out of state. It was the first time I'd lived with a man or moved out of my home state .He was adamant that he did not want to have kids and, crazily enough, I thought I could change his mind. Thinking I could change a man was such a crazy thought, but I didn't know any better. Our relationship came to a crossroads three years in. I considered packing my bags and moving back home. Most of my close friends had married and were having babies. I knew moving back home wouldn't be the same, so I stayed in my new home state. It was time to navigate this chapter of my life without the familiar peer or familial influence.

As I started dating again, I realized being 31 with no children and not being a divorcee was highly desired. Queue the goddesses; being different was finally paying off! I had a blast being on the dating scene again, I felt so empowered and started taking life one day at a time. That came to a screeching halt when I met and fell for a bald, white man, 14 years my senior and father to two teenage boys. He didn't want to have more children and a vasectomy left him unable. That was everything I didn't know I needed - it lifted a huge weight off of me. I could love him without pressure, knowing kids were off the table.

About three months into my new relationship, I received a text from my ex. It was a sonogram with the words, "I'd rather you hear this from me than see it on Facebook."

I felt my throat sink into my feet as I stood in the freezer aisle looking for my favorite butter pecan ice cream. The man that never wanted kids was having one and he wanted sympathy about this 'accident,' he had made. I had no sympathy to give. I had moved on with my life and was creating a life that was full of my own choices.

Declaring myself as a childfree woman being at the top.

I knew this was different, so I started talking about it instead of hiding it. Eight-year-old me needed to see a thriving woman speaking openly about choosing not to have children. I knew there were other women that needed to hear things like:

You don't need kids to complete you.

It's okay if you feel your biological clock doesn't have batteries and isn't ticking. Don't worry about the people that tell you that you'll change your mind. They can be wrong.

You aren't too young to know you don't want children.

Having kids doesn't mean your children will become your caretakers as you grow older.

And as I started opening up about my childfree choice, I connected with like-minded women. I found it helped other women feel seen, heard, and understood in their decision. Speaking out helped mothers with daughters that were making the childfree choice. They learned to embrace their daughter's stance instead of questioning it.

The Universe's plan for me to be childfree is for a bigger purpose. I am here to show women young and old; we have choices and we can embrace living a life that is real, raw, and free. When met with endless questions like:

"When are you going to have a baby?"

"Are you sure? You'll change your mind."

"What do you mean? You have to have kids."

I want women to realize that their choice needs no explanation.

Because it is my choice, is a valid answer. We don't have to scramble to explain why to someone that doesn't understand.

As women, we must learn to step into our truth and choice. This is where we find our true freedom and connect deepest to our purpose. All choices have their unique challenges. There is no competition in choosing motherhood or choosing to be childfree. My heart breaks for childless women whose bodies make the choice for them. That pain is devastating and I feel it in my childfree body.

At 36, I've never once bought a pregnancy test, been pregnant, or suffered the trauma of a miscarriage.

These things make me no less of a woman. They make me proud, unique, and in my truth. My eight-year-old vision of living in a home with kids that weren't mine has become my reality. I'm engaged to the man 14 years my senior, I have two step-children that look up to me, and I'm a crazy dog Mom to a 9lb ball of fluff.

Life is about finding that essence that's been tainted by the 'norms' of society. It's easy to lose ourselves in labels and forget the essence of who we truly are. Motherhood and being childfree are choices, not to be mistaken for our worthiness or identities.

Motherhood doesn't equal womanhood.

Yolanda, 36

To Be Frank

'I was raped.'

What do you imagine when you hear that sentence? A girl walking home alone at night being followed by a stranger? A slip of Rohypnol and a kidnapping perhaps? This is the rape narrative taught to us by our parents, school teachers and the media. We're told never to talk to strangers and always be on the lookout.

'Hold your keys between your fingers ready to use as a weapon.'

'Never wear headphones whilst walking alone.'

'Avoid dimly lit streets.'

'Call your friends as soon as you're home to let them know you are safe.'

But what if home is where you're most vulnerable?

I was raped when I was fourteen years old and the offender was by my first boyfriend.

He was in year 11. I was in year 9. He was tall, handsome, older and desirable. I was an ugly duckling, consistently overshadowed by my best friend who was smart, popular and incredibly sought after in the male department.

As a woman, it is ingrained within you that self-worth is directly associated with appearance, so it was all too fitting when one day I rocked up to class having had my braces removed, hair freshly dyed and sporting a brand-new outfit, that all of a sudden I began receiving the attention of a boy we'll call 'Frank'.

My parents were away on holiday, so with my newfound confidence I invited Frank over to watch a film. I thought we might make out afterwards. I shaved, just in case things went further than planned. I wasn't against the idea. In fact, as a young teen discovering my sexuality the thought of it was quite exciting. All I knew was that penetrative sex was not on the cards. It was a boundary I had put in place for myself and that line was not to be crossed.

I don't remember a lot from that night, but what I do know is that he never brought a film with him like he said he would, and burned into my memory is the feeling of his weight on top of me as I repeatedly pushed him away whilst uttering the word 'no' before eventually giving in, allowing him to destroy the threshold for which I held my self-worth, confidence and trust.

My parents found out. I was punished and called a stupid little girl. Irresponsible. Naive. Careless.

The shame I felt was overwhelming. I carried it around with me like a weight on my back while Frank resumed life as normal, free from the burden of his crime.

A week later he had moved on with a girl from the year above. I felt alone, misunderstood and confused. At this point I wasn't even aware I had been raped because in 2007, if you were in a relationship it was deemed normal to succumb to your partner's sexual needs, even if it was something you didn't want to do. Even if you verbally expressed non-consent. My situation was particularly confusing because I had been open to the idea of doing other sexual things, so surely that meant I was up for anything? The lines felt blurred and without the support of my friends and family I was filled with self-doubt.

Accepting that I was not to blame for what had happened took a long time and only really occurred due to stumbling across some rare articles on marital/spousal rape (which again, didn't initially resonate with me as the word marital suggested a long-term relationship and I was only fourteen and had been with Frank for less than a week). However, feeling like I finally had some support from strangers on the internet, I decided to confront him. Unsurprisingly, he denied it, invalidating my experience and making me appear dramatic and overly sensitive.

With one sentence he had catapulted me back to square one and my mind flooded with self-doubt yet again.

It's been fourteen years and I'm sure he hasn't given it a second thought. Without any kind of punishment or acceptance of his wrongdoing, why would that one insignificant night ever be at the forefront of his mind? For me, it took years to build back my confidence, and if I'm being totally honest I still don't fully trust men and I'm not sure I ever will. How can I when we live in a society where women are blamed for their behaviour? When we are the ones who are punished for their mistakes?

My entire experience would have been completely different had I had the support of my peers. It's not unusual for young girls to want to explore their sexuality whilst also having boundaries, and had I known this at the time I may not have spiralled into such a state of self-loathing.

Boys, I'm passing the mic to you. Educate each other, call each other out in times of injustice, and most importantly, own up to your mistakes.

I'm tired of your excuses, to be frank.

Rio, 28

42

<u>The caring one</u>

Today I am the caring one, the 'how are you feeling?' one, the problems are for sharing one,

The up and ready, bath is run, brush your teeth, let's make this fun,

The breakfast made, coffee down, what's the matter dear? no need to frown one.

Today I am the nose wiper, the school taxi driver, the 'have you got your bag, your coat?' one

The permission slip writer, the school welly finder, the be nice to Poppy - that's right, be kinder,

The rush back home to feed the cat, the defrost the tea and find Andy's lost hat.

The team manager in a busy role, the 'let's get this done' work takes its toll,

The get stuck in and through your emails, solving queries, picking apart tales,

The managing money, people and work tasks, the busy phone answerer, the 'have you got enough masks?'

Today I am writing the shopping list, the planning dinner, the nothing is missed,

the cleaner, the tidier, the parcel that's posted, the oven on, the chicken roasted

Today I am the must ring Nan, the 'is Grandad alright?' ' Did Andy insure his van?'

Does Summer need picking up, did she do well? Did I wash up her cup?

The lister, the reader, the queen of cuddles, the 'have you've hurt your knee splashing in puddles?'

I'll be the nurse too and rub it better whilst on the way to drop in that letter.

The on the phone if you need me there, the sock finder so that you have a pair,

the bath time clown making you giggle, the night time story reader - the dresser when your arms are in a pickle.

So when you're in bed and you're all tucked in, and I come downstairs and open the gin, understand that although I have crashed out, I'll do it all again without a doubt,

Because to me my dear womanhood is, indeed,
Being that superwoman that everyone doesn't know they need.

Hannah, 33

Crone

No longer a slave
To the waxing and waning moon
From a peaceful parapet
I peer through an experienced eye
With sadness at the world
With much to teach
From my accumulated years
Wrought from laughter and tears
Keeping my own counsel
A nurtured spirit abides
All is well inside
My internal mythology
Helps me stand my ground
Wisdom has found me
It was elusive in youth
Now, strong in truth
I realise that I cannot heal
A polarized world
But must remain true
to let my values unfurl
Kindness and succour to all
In abundant store
Squirrel like, preparing for old age
My maiden days are gone
But with hopeful heart
I carry on as sage
Faith, my breastplate
Charity, my three -legged stool
Love, my everything.

Mary, 52

My Daughter

With shaking hands, she traces the curve of her lips with the pencil following the instructions of the chirpy voiced young woman in the YouTube tutorial. The cherry-red bleeds over into the philtrum, and she lets out a frustrated groan before she erases the mistake with a swipe of a cloth and starts the painstakingly precise drawing again. She blots the excess of her finally made-up lips into the centre of a tissue, and she smiles at the imprint of her full red lips.

She raises her face to the mirror to critique the finished product, and I know, with the certainty of a mother's intuition, that her heart skips a beat at the image staring back at her.

It seems crazy that this is all she has ever wanted. So simple, and so reasonable. I think back to all the times we ask our children 'what do you want to be when you grow up?' and I wonder how many have never dared to whisper the very desires that are coiled deeply in their chest, holding in the very essence of who they are out of fear.

"How do I look?"

My eyes prickle with tears, and I swallow against the lump in my throat.

Everything she has done, everything she has been through, has been working up to this day. So much is on the line for her when she walks out of that door, and with it the knowledge that I can no longer protect her from the hatred and the danger that is almost statistically certain to come her way.

"You look beautiful." I tell her truthfully, and although I promised myself that I would remain strong when this moment came, I cannot stop the rush of tears that temporarily blind me.

"Oh, Mum!"

She hugs me, and even as I stretch my arms up and around her, I note with a smile that she carefully tilts her face to the side to avoid spoiling her handiwork.

"I'm sorry," I attempt to laugh at my surplus of emotion, pulling away to fan my blotchy, tear-stained face. "You just look so…" My voice catches in my throat, and I have to exhale deeply before I trust myself to finish. She is watching me through anxious green eyes, and I curse myself inside for not holding it together, and for adding to her nerves. "So yourself, my darling." I finally finish, before adding. "And so beautiful. You know that I'm so proud of you, don't you?"

Tears glisten in her own eyes, but she is stronger than me and she laughs, tilting her chin to the sky as if to tip them back into her body from where they had sprung. "You tell me every day, Mum."

When she has gone, I am unable to relax. My body feels too small to contain the torrent of emotions rushing through me as I wonder incessantly at where she is, and how her evening is going. Every fibre within me screams for her safety and knowing that I am no longer able to protect her from the cruelty and the dangers of the world reduces me from the fierce mother lioness to a vulnerable lamb. I remind myself for the hundredth time that this is her journey, and I must take a step back, but as I lie awake listening out for the sound of the door into the early hours, it's easier said than done.

"You look tired," my colleague comments the next day when I arrive at work.

"Teenagers," I smile, but already I feel my body stiffen in defence.

"Oh?" She raises an eyebrow, but I am wary to be drawn into conversation about my daughter's comings-and-goings knowing that the details will be rehashed and gossiped about in the staffroom at break.

It's laughable really when you think about the way they shame femininity, no matter the expression it takes.

Too weak. Too keen.

Too frigid. Too loose.

Too fat. Too thin.

Just a mother stripped of all previous qualities. Unnatural if you can't have or don't want kids.

Too ugly. Too self-obsessed.

Too dumb. Too opinionated.

Womanhood is a weakness, a disadvantage, and therefore to actively want all or any of it is a source of confusion, revulsion, suspicion.

Anger flashes like a flare in my chest at the thought, the injustice of these labels, and the history of repression as long as history itself.

Divide and conquer.

Repress through fear.

Control through confusion.

It was never about our weaknesses; it was always about theirs.

I haven't lost my temper yet, but I am very aware that it bubbles close to the surface; a cutting reprimand never far from the tip of my tongue. One day, I know that it will spill from me in the hot torrent of rage that threatens to overwhelm me when I feel their judgement in the air and in the little comments dressed up as concern.

"I don't know how I would feel about using the same toilets…"

"I've got nothing against them, it's just women need safe spaces."

"I mean, biologically we're very different, and you've got to agree that letting people who were born men into female sports is erasing…"

"I'm sorry," I want to say to the office gossips who I know talk about my daughter who used to be my son as if she is an episode of the mind-numbing reality television shows that they discuss around the coffee machine. "That so much of your personal identity is defined by your gender that my child being who they want to be is such a threat to you."

Because where it starts, and where it ends, for me is so much more simple than the arguments bandied back and forth like my child's human rights are up for discussion. The baby that I carried, birthed, and nursed reduced to the subject of a High School debate.

Why would you shame, or ostracize, my child for choosing the associations of this gender if you truly believed in equality?

You don't fear my child, who has never so much as raised a hand in violence, being in your space because she was born without the required vagina. You fear my child because she rejects the labels that you are conditioned to accept. No amount of what-about-ism will convince me of the transparency of your beliefs.

She is my child. She is a living, breathing, sentient being who is braver and stronger than you, with your hypothetical debates at the expense of her sense of belonging, will ever be. Because she has chosen to be her, not who she has been told she is by centuries of labels.

Lily, 38

On Opal Fruits and Love

It was 08:00am on a school morning and my mum was desperately scrubbing my scalp over the kitchen sink attempting to wash the purple food colouring out of my hair. I thought I looked quite good with my new punky vibe. It wasn't red like my heroine Toyah Wilcox, but it was the only food colouring in the cupboard other than blue and yellow. To my dismay, mum did a good job so I was left with one purple ear and a few patchy stains on my scalp for a few days.

I was 12 years old and well on my way to womanhood. My periods arrived at 10 years old, as did bra's and I was forever being questioned, "Have you been using my razor again?" my annoyed dad would moan with blots of tissue stuck to his chin.

My parents words, "Why can't you just be normal!" still sometimes ring in my ears, and believe me, I have tried! Being 'normal', what is that?

Fashion was not an option for me growing up. My dad was a milkman and my mum did several different part time jobs and had me, my younger sister and two older sisters to take care of too. We were a handful.

Our family income could not stretch to the ever changing societal 'fashion' trends. Ebay and internet bargains were not around 30 plus years ago, so I began to forge my own style. Admittedly this was in the form of neon tights and florescent odd socks, but hey, it fed a longing in me to be different and special. This felt like a rebellion against mainstream normal fashion, which in truth, although I secretly wanted to look like every one else, rebelling alleviated the pain of not being able to somewhat.

Hormones were coursing through my veins, freedom would call in the form of skiving school and spending many a day in the bright beckoning lights of the amusement arcades of Clacton-on-Sea.

Romance swirled up inside me from Disney films that translated into being snogged and worse by boys much older than me so that with each one who disappeared, another would come that I hoped this time would be Prince Charming.

The truth is, I was never really comfortable in my own skin and would go to great lengths to ease this discomfort.
When I tried tracing this back to a time and place where I first felt this 'comparing' myself to others, a strong memory came to mind.

I was 5 years old and my mum had volunteered to help on a school trip. As we were about to get on the coach, my mum said, "Oh look at that beautiful little girl." I looked up and saw Samantha. A little blonde porcelain doll-like girl, big blue eyes, tidy long curls swept back into an effortless ponytail. I especially remember experiencing shoe envy as she was wearing the most exquisite patent black shiny shoes with frilly ankle socks.

As we settled into our seats and mum gave me my packet of opal fruits for the journey, I asked her, "Am I beautiful mummy?" My mum paused and then said, "I wouldn't say beautiful, you're Tina." In my 5 year old mind, I came to the conclusion that prettiness might be a close second best to beautiful so I asked, "Mummy, am I pretty?"

My mum clearly didn't want to be having this conversation by her tone of voice and said, "You're not bad looking, just look out the window and stop it." I remember a heavy knot forming in my tummy, a kind of feeling being lost, tears prickling my eyes and a lump in my throat that even my favourite strawberry opal fruit struggled to get past. That was 43 years ago.

I am aware of this insecurity and have done much inner shadow work through counselling, Shamanic and Priestess training and very aware of when this wound gets poked and continue exploring how best tend to this whenever that happens. This feeling of 'not being enough', 'good enough' , 'beautiful enough', 'Whatever the blank is, not enough' has been a theme in different areas throughout my life to varying degrees.

I know without a doubt when this happens, because I feel triggered. I'll feel hurt, angry, resentful and usually self-blame or have imaginary arguments with the perceived person at fault and say all of the things I really want to say.

In my younger days... er... ok...maybe the most recent was last year... I would explode at whoever had intentionally or unintentionally poked at my wound which would usually send them reeling into shock as I'm not usually confrontational. A good friend gave me a mug which says, "I'm mostly love and light and a little bit go fuck yourself."

There's something here about that little 5 year old Tina being very much present in this 48 year old Tina. In fact, I would say my teenage Tina and all of my ages are present and all have different needs that only I know and more importantly - how to tend to them.

Social media has felt quite a flagellating experience with amazing looking women, perfect bodies, homes, careers, children, husbands, holidays and manage to keep all of their plates spinning effortlessly whilst sharing a yoga pose selfie or latest smoothie photo. I sometimes look at other women with both awe and envy simultaneously with how they manage their lives. Almost as though there is an unspoken expectation within for me to be more like them.

I'm single and was unable to have children, so a feeling of not being fully woman has crept in at times. The truth is, as my mum told me, I'm Tina, I'm me and I'm still on that journey of discovering who I am and loving and learning to accept all of me, all of the wounds, all of the beauty, all of the shadows and all of the light.

Others seem to act like mirrors, showing me where I need to give myself a little more tenderness, care and attention.

Even where I have experienced validation from others, there's also a recognition that although this may feel good or even uncomfortable, it all comes down to how I feel about myself, regardless of others perceptions.

I lost both of my parents in 2017. My mum to cancer in July and my dad in November to lung disease.

During that difficult year where they were no longer married and yet were both in their dying process, I was fortunate in that I was able to spend much time with them. It was a timeless time where the world fell away for a while and all that mattered was love, kindness, forgiveness and deep, deep presence.

I felt more raw, real and alive in that I felt every moment was precious, not only with my dying parents but with others too and with myself. Everything slowed down and my senses were heightened as my heart was cracked wide open.

In those times, I didn't care whether I was 'beautiful' or question if I was enough. All I cared about was love and all that mattered to me was to live from that place. I felt both excruciatingly vulnerable and immensely strong all at the same time. Everything took on a glow of raw beauty. The touch of my dad's hand holding mine whilst reading him stories of his beloved Cornwall.

My mums grace as she surrendered to personal care from hospice home carers. The days in which she recognised me and the nights when she was confused and asked me if my mother would be ok that I was visiting her so late. My parents passed away knowing and feeling how loved they were and I was left as an adult woman orphan knowing and feeling without a shadow of doubt that I was much loved too.

When I started to write this piece for this beautiful book, I had an idea of what I wanted to say and yet my parents seem to have both intervened and come in strongly during this process. Typing these last words I feel really moved. Feeling love for my parents and grateful for this opportunity to share my experience with you in this very moment.

I feel as though my mum wants to take my hand and go back in time to that school trip…After my mum shares her thoughts about how beautiful the other little girl is, we take our seats on the coach. She gives me my packet of opal fruits for the journey. As I unwrap my sweet, she says to me, "Ask me again".

I fiddle with my sweet wrapper nervously then take a deep breath,

"Mummy, am I beautiful?"

She turns to look at me and speaks with such love that my eyes sparkle and my heart skips and smiles as I settle deeper into my seat. As I look out of the coach window, I momentarily catch my own reflection and glimpse all the different ages of Tina smiling back at me as I swallow my favourite strawberry opal fruit, relaxing and softening into the journey.

Tina, 48

Just being me

When asked to speak about womanhood I was initially excited, thinking I can do this, I have plenty to say. However, when it came down to it, after three other attempts, I wasn't sure what to say. In my usual style, I was thinking too much about it: will people want to read what I write; is it really about womanhood; what does this say about me as a person? So now here we are: attempt number four to put something down on paper about this, and instead of thinking too much about it I am just going to write.

If I really think about what it means to me the answer that keeps coming up is that it means I am myself. I am a 30 something (will leave it at that) woman who lives in Texas with my wife, working in a completely male dominated field. I don't count myself as feminine nor do I count myself as butch. I don't follow fashions trends; instead I wear things that are comfortable and give me the confidence for that day to get what I need to do, done. Sometime that means it's jeans (or shorts, we are in Texas after all) a t-shirt, and a pair of converse; other times it's a smart pair of trousers, cute top, and some ballet flats, depending on where we are going and what we are doing. I probably only have two pairs of heels, three if you count the pair I bought for a ball and wore for a grand total of 20 minutes before kicking them off in favour of some flats, and I love both pairs. A shock to some people (although it irks me when they say that), is that I also own some dresses; I just don't feel comfortable wearing them unless it's for a special occasion. When we go out my makeup is simple but not worn every day, and I have a weird aversion to hair dryers, so my hair is dried naturally and usually tied back, which again for me is a comfort thing. I have had people in the past tell me they think I am not feminine enough or I dress too 'tom boyish,' but apart from the time I worked on a cruise ship and had to doll myself up, I have continued to stick to just being me.

Growing up we travelled a lot and moved around regularly as dad was in the army. This meant I spent a lot of time with my brother. He is older than me by 18 months and I spent countless hours playing with his toy cars, GI Joes (one of which was in love with my Barbie) and running around outside getting covered in mud playing soldiers with him and his friends. I also spent a lot of time playing with my Barbie dolls and doing crafty arty things, but I was never one for the really girly activities and I am incredibly grateful for my parents for not pushing them on me and allowing me to grow into the person I am now. When dad was either back for a few weeks from the Army, and then when he retired, he would spend his spare time either working on (or cursing at) the old Land Rover we had, or doing the house up, and that was prime father/daughter time for me. I would follow him around helping him make and fix things, always keen to know how he did something or if I could have a go. At the same time, I was also learning to cook, bake and sew (albeit badly on the sewing part) from mum and I fondly remember myself and my brother, with supervision from dad, cooking a meal for my mum's 30th birthday.

These skills followed me into adulthood, and I can say without a doubt my curiosity as a child -and the fact that I didn't care that while some of my friends where braiding hair and learning make up skills, I was mixing concrete not only shaped me as a person and allowed me to become independent but they also helped me get to a point where I am finally happy with my job. I have had some people say to me in the past that every woman should know how to cook and sew (notice I said woman not person) and I have even had people assume that because I am female, I have no clue when it comes to practical skills, so they take great pleasure in explaining to me the things I already know even if I didn't ask. It's my belief though that these skills are not gender specific, they are simply life skills that everybody should have the opportunity to learn.

Even though I am incredibly happy with where I am in life now - married, living in Texas with our dogs, surrounded by the most amazing group of friends - it can sometimes still be a challenge for others to accept me as I am, especially in the workplace. In my first job when we moved to Texas, working part time for the local government as an Environmental Technician, I gained a reputation thanks to the skills bestowed on me by my dad for being "The practical one."

I fixed the equipment, was very organized, could find my way around a database and oddly was the one happy to tidy up the office (I hate mess). Oh -and I had the fun task of trying to get the work truck running each Monday thanks to a dodgy battery. This was only a temporary seasonal job, though, and unbeknownst to me I had been "spotted" by another department head who was hiring just as my season was ending.

I had two options when I left that role: I could either work full time in an office-based customer service role similar to the many previous roles I held and didn't enjoy, or take a part time job that was practical, and based outdoors, and you guessed it, I went for the part time job. I was finally in a role that allowed me to excel at being me. The downside to taking that role was not that it was part time or that it was something I had never done before, it was that all of my colleagues were men who were mostly the same age as my dad, semi-retired, and 'just in it for the paycheck' kind of people.

I was told when I started that role that the last females to take it didn't last long, for various reasons, and it was soon very clear why. Some of these men were very set in their ways when it came to how they treated people, and I don't just mean women. It was everyone. Sexism and racism were rife, and the conversations were very politically charged. This meant that from day one I had the tough task of breaking through this, making sure I was not only able to confidently show them that women can do this role, but - ultimately- I showed that I could outperform them. There was no special trick to this, and I certainly didn't change anything about myself to fit in, they either accepted me as I was or not at all, and I was willing to call them out when they overstepped the mark.

It has taken a long time for some of them to accept me as I am, and, even a year in, some kinks are being ironed out, as they are very much set in their ways; but slowly each day I feel I make some progress on this. No longer do they feel they need to come to my rescue all the time when I am asked to deal with difficult situations; they know what I can handle and let me just get on with it. Some of them still try to mansplain things to me, and it's often those tasks I have done countless times and, in some cases, tasks they are unable to do themselves and I have even been told "I need a man's help, this is heavy work," when offering to help them out. All this being said, though, I still absolutely love my job, and many things about it and by sticking it out I have become a more patient person.

If I am honest, I think what has helped me turn this into something I love and look forward to going back to each week is that all through my time so far in this role I have finally been able to just be me.

Sarah, 37

Plants and Gardeners

Womanhood. Hmm, what does that word mean?

I've spent the last couple of weeks musing on different topics that encompass that word but kept realising that what and whom I was thinking about, would be better described as 'humanhood'.

In these days of gender fluidity, is it even okay to say 'womanhood', or have I just been living and working in Brighton too long???? (eye roll). Perhaps, I'm just over-thinking. There will be some friends and family nodding and laughing out loud by now!

Anyway, we are about to move house, having both retired (horrible word - now, there's another essay) to a West Sussex village and I have been thinking about how to make the house definitively ours. I was standing in M&S trying to resist buying some plants (non-essential in January 2021) when I thought, 'Eureka, that's it: plants!'

Humans are like plants: without roots they will topple; without nurture they will wither. What do plants need? Gardeners. What do I see when I look in the mirror, at my female friends, family and my two daughters? I see Gardeners.

Some of us can grow the seed, cocooning it within ourselves, but all of us can, and do, check the roots for stability whilst ensuring there is flexibility in the stem. Sometimes, we do this in spite of our own neglect; indeed, we can strive even harder to protect and empower. We feed, fertilise and enable blossoming. We prop them up; help them face the sun; sometimes we need to rein them in! As they grow, we can get scratched but we always need to 'handle with care'. The hardest part is to leave well alone, observe patiently, and stand back. Eventually, that bittersweet moment when they reach maturity and spread, faces facing forward, as they must if we've done a good job. (I did my best girls, honestly!)

Now, I'm not just talking about motherhood but also about how we are with our friends and family, and strangers, even. All of us are Gardeners, instinctively providing emotional nourishment; a helping hand removing the occasional thorn, opening our hearts to promise.

Very soon - well, actually I think we've already started - Di (soon to be my daughter's mother-in-law) and I will clasp our hands together around our two families, grafting them together lovingly, creating more new roots, and sharing our experiences to strengthen the ties.

To all my friends, family, the children I helped during 21 years in school, the new friends Di is sharing with me, but especially my two adorable, feisty, kind, intelligent Roses, I say, 'I hope I've been/am a good gardener; I always did/do my best. My very best'.

To any readers, I hope you enjoy reading this and find recognition; I know it's a bit flowery! Oops, sorry, I couldn't resist; I do like a good pun.

Colette, 61

Tulips

I starve myself for men who don't love me,
Don't eat for days so they can trace a finger down
The curve of my spine.
I starve myself for men who don't want me,
They want to feel like a man,
Primal with their arms curled round the stem of a tulip.
I starve myself for men who don't love me.
Don't eat for days to fit in a matchbox in their pocket.
I'm hollow and hungry.
Hands like feathers and a gossamer touch,
Mouth hungry,
Wanting,
I am a crescent moon waning.
The tulips have withered,
Stems snapped
And petals bruised and purple.
Their scent is sour,
No more a sweet smelling flower.
Their skin crackles as they fade.

Annouska, 26

Greenham Women

I didn't actually meet any of that small band of women who walked from Cardiff to the RAF base at Greenham in Berkshire in 1981 to protest at the decision to allow the Americans to hold Cruise nuclear missiles on British soil.

No, I didn't meet them but their actions, sacrifices and determination changed so many lives; mine and countless numbers of other women.

They empowered women; they influenced and gave hope and inspiration to other protests. And Cruise missiles did, eventually, leave.

I don't want to focus on the politics, economics or morals of the protest here. Vitally important, yes, and discussed and argued about constantly: around camp fires; at meetings... everywhere!

But...

This was where we grew, individually as women, growing in confidence, learning new skills. In groups, to open up about ourselves and share ideas and skills. I learned to appreciate women whose lives were so different from mine. I also learned to voice my irritation or anger at someone instead of keeping silent and sulking.

Telephone trees to communicate! Radical eh?

And realised that, as a movement, we could change situations.... peacefully. Not to be riled by the cheap jibes by some of the police who laughed and shouted to us to carry on as we were paying for their summer holiday. Not to respond as we were physically intimidated by police horses being ridden directly at us. How to use the non-violent strategies we had been taught by other women, such as being passive and leaden when being moved. And what our rights were if we were arrested or detained.

I already had some experience of demonstrations and protests. I had marched, as a student, for student grants. I had protested about A Woman's Right to Choose. I was a member of a consciousness raising group. But coming together with so many other women, of every age, class and sexual identity at the same time was so uplifting, so celebratory, so challenging!

Greenham memory:

Driving down the motorways from Yorkshire on a Friday evening after work. 12-15 of us in a Transit, heading to Greenham for the weekend. A motley crew. Moira, a really lovely middle-class lady who was always perfectly groomed, perfectly made up, who brought her battery portable carmen heated hair rollers with her. She chain smoked as she stood at the fence for hours calmly, repeatedly telling the impassive, robotic American soldiers that she was doing this for children and grandchildren everywhere.

The sharper edged members of the sisterhood whom I loved but who sometimes were so relentless and certain in their views that I could feel irritated by or inadequate to them. We learned to work together. We were simply not going to stop. However we looked and behaved at the beginning of the weekend, by the end we were tired, cold, dirty, sometimes exhilarated, sometimes frustrated and down or angry. But we were still resolved in our determination. How on earth did the women staying for long periods deal with all of this???

Greenham memory:

Cold, wet, dark. Having to put the tent up quite near 'the shit pit' as there was no other space. Woke up in the grey early morning light to a sodden sleeping bag where the tent had leaked. What was I doing here?

Greenham memory:

A woman playing the violin, very badly, while I was trying, very badly, to do the shoulder stand on uneven ground. We both end up giggling and go and try and find a cup of tea!

Greenham memory:

Embrace the Base. Women, from all over, gathered in our thousands to hold hands and encircle the perimeter fence Laughing, singing, crying. Silence. And then a single voice begins the refrain which we all take up echo, over and over. This still sends shivers down my spine. A cold, ghostly grey day and our voices permeating the mist:

"You can't kill the spirit
She is like a mountain
Old and strong
She goes on and on…"

Sue, 69

Love Story

This is a (sort of) love story about a girl and her body.
The most intimate relationship a woman will ever have is
between herself and her body. It's the one constant thing
throughout her life, from the beginning to the end. And
although it goes through many changes over the years, it will
be the one constant, for better or worse, richer or poorer, in
sickness and in health. But we all have at least one especially
troublesome part.

If you ask anyone who knows me what my defining physical
trait is, chances are it won't be my big brown eyes, my goofy
smile or my ever-changing hair colour. It will more than likely
be my giant bum. I have, in fact, been identified solely on this
one feature many times. I've been greeted from behind by
people (men to be specific) who I haven't seen in several
years calling out things along the lines of "Oi, Lorna! I'd
recognise that arse anywhere!" more times than I would care
to admit.

My journey with acceptance, like many others, has been a long
and rocky one. From a young age, I struggled to form a
connection between what I thought and was told I should look
like, and what the mirror showed me.

I remember being around 7 or 8 years old and being told that I
had "childbearing hips", "a womanly figure" and various other
comments about being "curvy". To me, whose teen idols were
the likes of Gwen Stefani, Mischa Barton and Winona Ryder,
these ideas were horrifying. They became very problematic
and formed a complex which would take years to break down
and eventually embrace. Before I even began secondary
school, I was already wearing women's size 10 trousers, I felt
humiliated, like I belonged in a freak show; a little
melodramatic, of course, but how I felt nonetheless. All I
wanted was to look like the other girls my age, the girls in the
magazines. It always felt like people were looking, and often
they were.

Like many other girls and women, I've been plagued by catcalls and unsolicited comments from total strangers throughout my life, starting in my very early teens. It left me feeling insecure and somewhat inhuman, just something to be leered at and objectified by men. Was I a whole human being with a personality, thoughts and emotions? Or was I just a fine piece of ass? I considered many drastic options, from changing my eating habits to incredibly invasive surgery to change my body, to make myself what I saw as more attractive.

I truly thought that would be how things were forever, that I would never be comfortable in my own skin but, as they always do, the tides eventually turned. Out went the Kate Mosses and Paris Hiltons with their super skinny, waifish frames, and in came the Beyoncé's and Kim Kardashians. Big butts were beautiful. Women were finding ways to exaggerate and pad out their bums. They wanted to look like me.

My point is that societal norms change over time. Beauty standards come and go. The media will always try to trick us into thinking what we are is "less than". The ideals that I grew up struggling to adhere to throughout the 90s and 00s have evolved into something new, as they undoubtedly will do again and again, just as they always have done. The main thing I've realised is that womanhood encompasses all who want to be defined by it, regardless of size, shape, colour, or any other factor and that the most important thing is to accept you for you. We shouldn't have to force ourselves into an aesthetic ideal but embrace and love what we have. It's certainly not easy, I have spent many tear-filled sleepless nights begging the universe to "fix" me, but it is possible with patience, perseverance, and - honestly - learning not to give a fuck.

It took time but eventually, I gained an understanding that my body is what it is and that it's mine, and mine only. Catcallers and oglers no longer faze me; I now feel confident enough to confront them and have even been known to make men who stare too long pay for a photo. I dress how I want and not "for my body type", whether that be cute little dresses, joggers or skin-tight latex trousers.

I've battled with the expectations that I thought the world had for me, I've fought the inner voice in my head and, for now, at least, I think I've kind of won. These days we coexist peacefully, my giant arse and I, mostly happy in the space we take up.

Lorna, 29

<u>Suzi Q does gender</u>

A lot of what I am writing is in my autobiography UNZIPPED. But it must be said, being written from a now 70 year old perspective.

I began my existence in this world in Grosse Pointe Woods, a suburb of Detroit, Michigan on June 3, 1950, the second to the last of 5 children: 4 girls and 1 boy. Being one of 5 makes it essential, especially wired like I am, to find your voice, and even more important if you are female. Which is a dichotomy for me because I have never really done gender, not since a very young girl. But this book which I have agreed to appear in, means I must tackle this issue. So here I go.

I have 3 sisters who err on the side of 'feminine'. They do make-up, they do girly clothes, hair do's, etc. I was always and still am the tomboy of the family. And, before you jump to the conclusion that I 'became' the tomboy just to find my voice, nope, it was just me. I was a square peg in a round hole, and it made me who I am.

My mother. Where do I start with this remarkable women? She had 8 pregnancies, bore 5 children, and also took in a total of 9 orphans through the years. She made her entire life, her brood. As my dad was fond of saying 'if your mother had both legs chopped off, she would still drag herself through broken glass to get to any of you". Dramatic it may be, but true.

So, I grew up watching this woman of her time, with all its female rules, regulations, and expectations, doing nothing but cleaning and cooking, doing the washing, taking us to the doctors, dentist, school: every job you can think of, she was there. The floor in the kitchen was so clean you could eat off it. Your clothes were washed, dried and ironed and in your room every morning. There was a different healthy meal every evening promptly at 5 p.m. And there were the walks we took, no matter what the weather was, rain, snow, storm... it didn't matter, we took our daily walk.

In the evening after our allowed T.V. time and bedtime looming, she would climb the stairs and tuck us in bed, until we reached the grand old age of 7. Then, as she told each one of us, 'you are old enough to take yourself to bed now.' That night was the loneliest night of my childhood, climbing up the stairs by myself. Since she has been gone, 1992, I have been climbing up those stairs alone every single night. Somehow, though, I can feel her walking beside me.

As I reached my teens, and started my first all girl band with my sister, two other sisters and a neighbourhood girl, I started to see a completely different side to my mother, and got to know the person. Often I would sit with either a band member or a friend at the kitchen table and my mom would start to talk. She was fascinating to listen to, about her own early life in Illinois and then to Detroit, with her Hungarian parents.

They were not well off, and lived very frugally. One of her siblings, a little girl, had an illness that required sugar. She got very ill one evening, so my mom's father went out to see if anyone had some sugar for him. By the time he came back, the child had died. They had another boy, blond haired and beautiful, according to my Grandma Sanisly. He was playing outside in the snow with his friends, and when it was time to come back, he decided to climb over the fence. The woman next door had a gun, and she shot him. Somebody came to the family home to alert everyone; my grandmother said she will never forget the sight of her boy lying in the white snow surrounded by blood. And the reason? "He was stealing my chickens." Unbelievable but true. My grandfather (who I never met) never got over this. They didn't have enough money to take it to court.

She also talked about her hopes and dreams as a young girl.

"I could have been a writer. When we had to do a book report on a book we had read, I simply would make one up. It was so good, the teacher asked me where I got the book from!"

"I could have been a comedian, just like Phylis Dillar; I have exactly the same kind of ability."

And then talking about love:

"I went out with a doctor for a few years before I met your dad. I often wonder how my life would have turned out had I married him instead"

Which leave you wondering if she was 'satisfied' with her lot. She loved us all unconditionally, but what a price. To have no life of your own. To never reach goals, to never dare to dream.

One thing sticks out in my mind as pivotal to my development and attitude to life.

It was Sunday, usually the only day my dad didn't do evening gigs, although sometimes there was an afternoon one. Anyway, grocery shopping day was on Monday. I saw my mom in the kitchen put her hand out for my dad to give her the money for this. Innocent and necessary as it may have been, I did not see it that way. I made up my mind there and then that I would NEVER put my hand out to anybody; that I would make my own way and be responsible for myself. I have stuck to that my entire life.

Everyone who has had the pleasure of knowing my mom says the same thing: friends, boyfriends, ex-husbands... doesn't matter. This is her legacy. She was special, compassionate, warm, loving, and one of the most decent people ever.

I am very much her daughter in many ways, but in truth, I can't shine her shoes.

I wrote her a poem (from my poetry book, Through My Eyes), had it printed out and framed it. She hung it on her wall. Next time I visited, there was a different picture in it.

"Where did the poem go mom?"

"I changed it; it was such a waste of a pretty frame."

Wow - that says it all.

My legacy is that I was the first 'female' rock and roll singer and musician to have worldwide success, thereby changing the game plan. The truth is, I kicked down the door because I didn't see the door. And even though I am 'non' gender, I am proud to be a woman, and proud to carry on my mother's example. It's all about strength. It's all about finding the light inside. It's all about being the best YOU, you can be. Here is the poem I wrote.

A Mother

A mother's face
One more cradle to rock
A mother's place
Cold heart to unlock
Day after day
No pleasure in sight
Is there no way
To ease her plight
A silent space
No door to knock

A lonely smile
Sweeps her broom
Dust of emptiness
Fills the room
Pictures of children
Share the wall
Night after night
Shadows fall
On barren seeds
Within her womb

A mother's face
So soft to touch
Was it my disgrace
I needed so much

Suzi, 70

The (temporary) end of me

When I was asked to do this I was excited but a little apprehensive. A woman's journey through life is deeply personal and any anecdotes or horror stories that happen along the way can be quite an intimate thing to share. I am painfully honest about most things in my life with those that know me; that being said there is usually only a certain amount of truth in that honesty. It's only in recent years that I have truly learnt that IT IS OKAY NOT TO BE OKAY and to talk about it, but even now it's a battle.

At the age of 31 I'm only just starting to work it all out, what my worth is, what I deserve and what I want from my life.

Admittedly, it's a slow process but I'm getting there. For most of my adolescence and twenties I put all my worth in what others thought of me and the attention that I received from men. Outwardly I guess I would have seemed very confident, fun loving and self assured but the truth couldn't have been further from that. I got myself into more bad situations and relationships than I can count but was always unable to break the cycle of my own toxic behaviour.

Then, at age 27 on a Tuesday evening, I was taken to the Walk In Centre and my life really took a turn. I had the worst flu I've ever had and terrible sciatica. An hour after arriving I was seen and the doctor turned to me and said "I think you're pregnant"

I didn't literally pass-out but my mind went completely dark, the lights were on but no one was home. Other than being sick I don't remember most of what happened in the 5 minutes that followed. I was sent to maternity where I sat with my equally dumbstruck parents and waited for a scan. After what felt like hours I received a speedy scan and the doctor confirmed it: "Yup, there's definitely a baby in there"

FUCK.

How? I took the pill, I even had regular periods. Why did my body lie to me? Why did biology lie to me?! I already hated my body and this certainly didn't improve our relationship.

I was admitted straight away to be assessed the following day, but the stress and shock sent me into labour less than an hour later. The morning rolled around - as did the staff changeover. My new midwife for the day happened to be one of my ex's mothers. Less than ideal and bloody typical of my luck but it turned out she was exactly what I needed (she's also an incredible midwife and a marvellous woman!).

After spending most of a day being told to push a human out of my vagina after having my water broken (which is a wholly unpleasant experience) and whilst in a somewhat shocked and absent state, I just couldn't do it anymore. I was overwhelmed, terrified and totally lost. Broken. Even though all of my family were around me I felt totally alone. Alone, afraid and if I'm honest embarrassed that I found myself in the situation at all. Eventually I was given an epidural and c-section. I have very few memories of this; being taken to surgery and shaking uncontrollably is one that stands out, probably not as much as when they cut me open and said "it's a girl. Oh, hang on, there's another one"

ANOTHER ONE...FUUUCK!

The next thing I remember clearly is waking up back in my room (still shaking), my incredible midwife pushing me in the shower and asking if I wanted to see the twins. Now, this was terrifying. I had never wanted children, now I had two.

I'd heard a lot of people say it but feeling it yourself is powerful: the moment I saw them I loved them more than anything else, I didn't know what day it was or what the hell I was going to do but the terror and doubts I'd been filled with moments before had lessened.

It was shortly after I got home that I truly hit rock bottom.

Now, given what I've literally just said that might seem like a really bizarre thing to say especially as welcoming babies is usually quite a joyous event, but this completely changed my whole world in 24 hours. I had completely lost who I was as a person. I suppose the best way to describe it is that I was drowning in grief for the person I used to be. The waves of depression and anxiety would crash over me and looking back it was most likely post-natal depression but I was unwilling to deal with any of it or even acknowledge it. I pushed it all down and kept going. Eventually I slipped back in to bad habits, smoking, a weekly binge drinking session and men. All the while being a single mother and struggling to deal with my reality. Using alcohol and men to make myself feel better or like my old self but usually it just made things much worse. I wasn't happy before and I definitely wasn't now.

I always remember people saying "make the most of it, they grow up so fast" but I could rarely enjoy motherhood and anytime I did relish in it, the guilt of not feeling that way all the time would creep in. This is one of my biggest regrets.

I desperately wanted to be okay but I didn't know how to make it happen or who to turn to. I was already feeling isolated and terrified. I kept the arrival of my children very quiet. It was something I simply didn't know how to explain, I knew people would constantly be asking "but how didn't you know?" and I definitely didn't have an I answer; all I had was fear of the judgement that I had already seen on others faces and I knew my mental health couldn't take it. I confided my feelings in a few of my closest friends and just saying it all out loud was an unbelievable relief. Don't get me wrong, it's not a quick fix kind of situation and breaking the cycle of toxic behaviour takes a long time, but making that first scary step is pretty freeing.

Through most of this time I always found myself circling back to the same thoughts: Why is there so much pressure to be a certain kind of parent? Why is there so much judgement? Why can't I fit into that box? It's easy now to say that you don't. You don't have to fit any mold.

But the monumental pressure I felt from others expressing opinions or telling me I was "doing it wrong", from social media and the media in general, it was easy to feel like a constant failure.

I'm now 5 years down the line and as I finish writing this I am curled up under a blanket with my beautiful children (who are driving me crazy!); although it may be taking me a while to put the pieces back together, smaller steps are what I needed. After such a traumatic event, I don't handle change well and struggle if I can't control a situation (our current climate has certainly been one of self discovery and self improvement for me!). I still suffer quite intense but short swings of depression and anxiety but I am now not ashamed or afraid of it, I have learnt ways to cope.

I have a partner that loves, respects and understands me and what it is to be a parent (he calls me on my bullshit too and that's pretty important!). I am more confident and less self conscious, I spend less time feeling like I'm suffocating while I'm out in public. I'm not as hung up on my appearance; my relationship with my body is definitely still love/hate but that particular relationship is probably the most damaged one and a whole other story.

I guess the relationship that all of this made me work on the most was my relationship with myself. I was raised in a traditional household and was never really exposed to any other kind of upbringing. The constant shame and guilt I felt, and sometimes still do feel, was unbearable at times over a situation that I didn't have any control over. The stereotypical views of "what a mother should be," with the stigma of being a single mother weighing down on me and crippling my mental health even further. The constant feeling of judgement, even from your own family, was so detrimental and most people would say "just ignore it" but learning to do that is quite a skill and I have a lot of respect for those that can. Having amazing friends and a supportive partner - all of whom I can turn to and confide in and have lift me up - is undoubtedly what's made things easier for me.

Sharing my story and connecting with others is something I've been reluctant to do in the past, but letting go of some of my guilt and shame has allowed me the peace of mind I needed. I'm writing this in the hope that it could help someone else and they might see there is a light at the end of the pain. It may not be relatable to you personally, but I always think the ability to understand another's pain is a wonderful gift.

Time is a healer and while my life is now probably what would be considered boring, I am happier (and more exhausted) than I've ever been. Being a woman is very complicated, but I guess the same could be said of any sex, no matter who you are or what your story is.

Laura, 31

Living our purpose

This is the first time in my career spanning over a decade and a half that I had to work from home. While the concept had been fronted in many places, in the service industry I work in, it was unheard of to work from home. Actually, in our country it wasn't even that common until Corona happened. A few months into the pandemic then we were required to work from home. It made sense because it reduced the chances of infection by a big margin.

Now working from home seems like such a simple thing. You know, just take your laptop and start working. Ideally you are just changing the work station. I wish it was that simple.

First there is the issue of time management. You don't have to wake up early to beat the traffic after all you are a few steps away from your work station. You can literally wake up a few minutes to 8.00 a.m. and make it for the morning meeting. This effectively means you sleep more in the morning. You stop dressing up and, in my case, working out. My entire morning routine was totally disrupted.

Pre-Corona I would work out at 5.00 a.m. then prepared to be out of the house by 6.30 to make it to work. Now, this did not make sense no more. I found I woke up half an hour before 8.00 a.m. to shower then get seated at my home desk. This also took a lot of discipline because sometimes you found yourself struggling to get out of bed.

The evenings were strange too. While when physically going to work meant that you had to be conscious of the evening so as to beat the traffic home, here you are two minutes away from your bedroom. You find yourself working longer hours since there is no pressure to go home.

Secondly is the fact that you stop wearing what we call work clothes and shoes. You end wearing pajamas or track suits all the time. One day you try to wear a skirt and it just will not go past your bust neither can you wear it from the bottom. I had gained too much weight and I did not notice it coming.

The fact that I didn't move much kind of stuck to the same radius then again, my morning workout routine was disrupted. Also, I had time to eat all my meals at home. In the office sometimes there happens to be no time to eat or no food. Even shoes do not fit. My feet were not accustomed to being free restricting them to shoes is now painful. These changes are not even noticeable until when you try the clothes and shoes on.

Thirdly for me was this was the first time I opted not to have a nanny for my child. I talked to her and asked whether she was ready to take up some chores and also take a break from someone minding her all the time. In any case, she was now in senior school. She accepted.

Adjusting into it was a bit tough. I prefer us eating meals at scheduled times. This did not always work as sometimes my workload spilt into my cooking time and hence, we ate later than expected. My child could also sometimes delay in doing tasks e.g. washing dishes. Sometimes they could get washed 6 hours after they were used. Sometimes she wanted to escape some tasks e.g. washing her shoes.

I guess having not done these things before sometimes gave her comfort that she should not be doing them. We struggled in the beginning then we picked a rhythm somewhere after about a month. It was also for me the discovery or perhaps a reminder that children and even grown-ups me included don't just take into performing tasks. You repeatedly insist they do them until it becomes routine.

I also realized my child is not perfect actually she is just a child. She will still tell me that her milk is too hot despite the fact that I am in the middle of a meeting. She will ask for her face towel when I am cooking instead of looking for it. She sometimes will ask to see who are the other participants in our meetings or will ask me to put on my video for her to greet my colleagues. A child she is, hence expect childish behaviours. I have graciously accepted it.

My child was taking online classes. I think we were not cut out for it. Balancing between my job and monitoring school activities was something else. Following up to ensure they logged in and actually learnt rather than played games or just stared outside. Sometimes her French classes started and she absolutely had no idea where her books were or started sharpening her pencils when the class was on. It was impossible to understand how she did not find it important to be prepared for her classes. I was keeping up being an employee and now a part time teacher. The last duty was not exactly my forte.

You know what I have learnt in the last few months from my experience?

I am not super woman, far from it. Actually, I don't even desire it. I am okay with what I have. I am okay if we eat a hot meal and an hour late from what I perceive as dinner time. I am okay with average clean especially if it me doing the cleaning. Our house needs to be habitable for us. Dishes can delay being washed for another half hour nothing will really happen. I allowed our home to be just that a home for my daughter & I and that is okay. My daughter has also blossomed when I loosened the rules. I guess she also enjoyed the freedom of not imaging that we were hospitality experts.

I also learnt to have expectations that are realistic and achievable. It is okay sometimes to be number two. I cannot be everything to my daughter. She is also not everything to me. We also like very different things and have a different outlook on things. I do get tired and annoyed. My child is not perfect, neither am I. There will be hugs, laughs and celebration. There will be tears, apologies and sighs. We are those people they talk about as square pegs in round holes – non-conformists and we are okay with that. We are just trying our best and that is good enough, anything more is likely to be a disaster.I learnt we are just human meeting our purpose on earth. We are grateful to be down here and healthy.

Nyambura, 39

My Superwomen

Picture the scene. It's the third national lockdown in less than 12 months. I am self-isolating, currently recovering from a migraine, and listening to music that evokes nostalgia. I am sat here thinking of my closest friends: cue Alicia Keys, circa 2009.

I don't have any sisters by blood, but I did grow up with seven Superwomen to love and be loved by, to fight with and fight for. These seven fierce females are an extension of my identity as an individual; they've been with me since I knew what it meant to have friends.

We were born in the Eighties and there are eight of us in our friendship group, so naturally we refer to each other as Eighties Ladies. I know. It's an ingenious name for our enduring collective. Before I go any further, this is not an attempt to rip off a Sex and The City episode; I am not going to expose our sexual conquests or fashion faux pars, however tempting it might be. Plus, it is unrealistic to attempt to summarise decades of stories, events, and memories in this short article. Instead, I am going to try to capture for you how my Superwomen have contributed to my sense of womanhood.

I grew up in a small sailing town on the Essex coast and was fortunate enough to meet my oldest friends at nursery school and we found the rest of our BFFs at secondary school. It was during our college lunch breaks though, usually in the drama studio or in my mum's sunroom, that our friendship really blossomed. These are the girls who have been with me throughout it all: from the messy, emotionally fraught, adventurous, and perplexing teenage years to this current day.

When we were in our teens, Friday night couldn't come quick enough and spending time with my besties talking about boys, body image, and what we had planned for the weekend was a fundamental part of my existence. Typical weekends in our early 20s were spent getting ready for nights out dancing, whilst listening to our pre-drinks playlists and playing games.

From our late teens until our early thirties, every Tuesday evening meant 'girls' dinner', where we'd take turns hosting a meal and catching up on our week.

Halloween meant a theme for dressing-up, a pumpkin carving competition, and busting out some freaky poses for photos. Christmas heralded the little black dress and time to grab some cocktails, as well as a night in wearing fluffy socks and a festive sweater, whilst stuffing our faces, watching Mean Girls, and giggling about the not-so-secret, secret Santa gifts – oh! the year of three butter dishes was priceless. Birthdays, weddings, baby showers, or an ordinary day of the week, it doesn't matter what we are doing, we can still lose time talking over each other as we put the world to rights.

At 34, the Fridays come and go like they're on Red Bull and getting all eight of us in one place for several hours is more of a challenge than ever thanks to adulting. Although, no matter how much time passes, that one photo still resurfaces every year to get us all using the 'laughing crying' emoji face multiple times, whilst simultaneously experiencing real world face ache.

pauses to reflect and find that photo

It feels like yesterday that we were on our first girly holiday sunbathing with a hangover and yet we've come a long way since our friendship began. Multiple memories come rushing back to me and I can't help but smile, even at the ones that make me cringe and feel a pang of "Urgh. I was such an idiot at times". All of those experiences were incredibly important because they taught me that whatever happens, my Superwomen will be there - in one way or another.

Like when I slipped and fell into the sea at night, or when I travelled to Thailand, or when I needed a lift to a group therapy session, or when I was being messed around by a guy, or when I got confirmed, or when I needed volunteers for my research, or when my dad died, or when I got engaged – they've had my back throughout so many important moments of my life. These ladies will be with me always and forever.

I am not sure how or when Eighties Ladies was actually formed and I am not sure when I realised that these seven magnificent individuals would stick by me through anything and everything, but I do know how they make me feel. Aristotle got it right: "The whole is greater than the sum of its parts": each individual dynamic relationship contributes to the fabric of our friendship group. Like a patchwork quilt, each section wouldn't keep you warm on its own; the patches are much more effective when sewn together. As we hit our thirties, I certainly appreciated on a new level that friends like mine are not a 'given' and that an unbreakable bond like ours is actually pretty rare and extraordinarily special.

Ok, I need to illustrate this further for you.

When I decided to move to South Korea for a year, I was not in a particularly strong place emotionally or mentally and I was certainly not connected to the space within myself that Michael Neill refers to as innate wisdom. I told myself I should seize the day and travel to the other side of the world because, well, I thought I was taking control of my life rather than running away from my problems. Hmmm... Hindsight is a wonderful thing.

When I look at the photos of the send-off my Eighties Ladies gave me that summer - including a mix CD I cherish to this day - I see so much joy and love, despite the fact I was still reeling from my dad's diagnosis of early-onset dementia the year before and felt desperate to escape the mounting pressure and consuming heartache his illness brought me.

Inevitably, I returned to the UK within a month and my girls were there to support me during my darkest time, along with my family. At this junction, many other friends faded away. However, my Superwomen stuck by me, which couldn't have been easy for them to do because I was numb and withdrawn. I know it must have been tough to watch as I made a mess of being me for a while. As I was searching for a light at the end of the tunnel, feeling alone and disconnected, I was loved unconditionally and reminded regularly that I am Superwoman.

It isn't all about what my Superwomen bring to my life though. I know my significance in their lives too: my freshly baked triple chocolate brownies are amongst my many endearing qualities. Seriously though, it was an incredible honour to be asked to be a Godmother almost 12 years ago, to the firstborn child of our friendship group. I cherish the days out I have had with my Goddaughter over the years: watching films at the cinema, tobogganing, painting ceramics, jumping off inflatables in the sea, climbing rope ladders in trees and talking about growing up.

The value I place on my role in helping her grow into a kind, smart and secure young lady cannot be easily articulated. One day, all too soon, she will want to spend days out with her own Superwomen, instead of with her Godmother. In fact, each of the incredibly precious mini versions of my Superwomen make me feel doubly blessed to have our friendship group and I cherish the next generation of us. Now we have family days out, as well as girly time.

Even when we are separated, like during an unprecedented global pandemic, we always have each other. Of course, we utilise every possible social media platform to help tide us over until we are able to see each other in person. Daily contact - however fleeting - means we are able to be part of each other's lives continuously, even if it is just to send an absurd number of snaps because we love using the bunny ears filter.

How do you maintain a friendship for decades? All relationships require effort, that's no secret, but our bond is a powerful force enhanced by our ability to be ourselves, trust and accept each other, and love one another regardless. As I navigate different stages of my life, my Superwomen help affirm my sense of identity and belonging; I am eternally grateful for our unique and irreplaceable connection.

"Even when I am a mess, I still put on a vest with an 'S' on my chest - Oh yes! I am a Superwoman" - Alicia Keys

Rebecca, 34

Fragments of my love

You're the crisp air after a storm.
The first breath after being trapped under a wave.
Rain that makes cars clean and the world fresh again.
You're that green English countryside, with its valleys and its
history and its untapped glory.
You are everything good about mankind.
You are extremely humble, immeasurably gifted;
Your kindness is deeper than the ocean and your patience,
wider than it.
You are perfectly strong and unimaginably wise and so, so
handsome.
Yes, you have some dark clouds and corners too, yet I love
you all the more.
Maybe my love is blind or a little bias?
But I know my love for you is stronger than I've ever known,
deeper than I thought possible and more passionate than I've
ever dreamed of.
So much of life hinges on that which we have no control over.
So I plea we the heavens on a regular basis to keep breath in
your lungs, because if your chest were to ever stop rising, my
heart, my being would freeze over.
I'll vow to love you, walk with you, give myself to you.
I vow to strengthen you through the valleys of life.
Over the mountain tops, through storms of test and trial;
whether our days overflow with joy and happiness, or we are
stumbling through streets of wreckage.
I will love you passionately, purely, fiercely, simply, wildly.
And I will always love you faithfully.
In times of victory and in times of trouble, I'm on your side.
I'm in your corner, supporting and fighting with you,
encouraging you to be the incredible man that God has made
you.
I will honour and love you until the breathe in my lungs runs
out.

Elle, 31

Loving a father

I don't think I ever expected to fall in love with a man who had a child in a previous relationship and to make things more complicated, for that child to live in his home country when he was living in mine.

But here I am at 28 years old having moved to a new country during the corona virus pandemic so my partner can see his daughter on a regular basis.

Firstly, I should say I'm incredibly lucky that his daughter loves me and that his previous partner is lovely, and we all get on very well; after all the child comes first. Even his daughter's grandparents on her mother's side have been completely wonderful in helping me settle into a new country and lifestyle which I am eternally grateful for.

However, having a daughter from a previous partner may have also been the biggest challenge to our new relationship. I'd have ideally been the first person he'd have thought of in the day and that I was number one priority (even just for a small while). After all, this was how my past relationships had started. But starting a relationship with someone who has a child, you will never be their first priority. There's a reason you can't just fly away on a couple's holiday and there was always someone else to call, even on a weekend away.

As a woman, I've always had an idea of how I wanted to raise my own children but, in this situation,, it is not for me to say how he should raise his daughter. You can't change what has happened and how they have been brought up and it's certainly not your responsibility or right to change how they are being raised now. It's a matter of opinion and as long as the child is happy and healthy that's really all I can ask. It also makes your wonder about having your own children one day. Will our child be second best to his first child? Will I be able to raise my child the way I had hoped? Will this child be okay with us having a child of our own? Will this relationship expire and leave me a single mum? This wasn't my life plan.

Don't get me wrong; his daughter is wonderful, intelligent, loving and beautiful. She's like a best friend and always wants to chat and play with me. It gives me a sense of purpose and something to focus on when I'm alone in a new country and she teaches me new things as I teach her. I really do love her and couldn't imagine her not being around.

I can honestly say it's been a massive learning curve, but I will take each day as it comes, try to be the best role model I can and do my best to put my frustrations and irrational thinking aside. I will always try and think from her own mother's point of view and never get in the way of his daughter's relationship with her Mum. Being a female influence in his daughter's life is incredibly important to me but I already feel pressures to be a care giver and maternal figure, and I wonder if this is unique to the female experience or if this is a stepfather's experience this too? I guess I only can talk from my own experience. I certainly never thought I would be thrown into a Mother role so early in a relationship, but now I am here I really wouldn't have it any other way.

Lorna, 28

Bayonets & Daffodils

The year is 1990. My 20 year old mother is 7 months pregnant with me. It's 4am, 6 degrees outside, and she's trying to get some sleep in a cramped cut and shut Ford Escort. Legally, she owns a home with my biological father, her then husband; in reality her husband's lost his job, drinks and loses his temper so the car's a safer place for the night.

This is the reality for a lot of women. Not necessarily the violence but the fact that on paper they share in the equity but in reality they gaze longingly at what's rightfully theirs through a frost-coated window.

Growing up, my mum was, in a word, stretched. At one point she worked three jobs on top of raising me as a single mother. All children are blessed with a selfishness, myself included; that means they extend no sympathy to the various scaffolds from which our parents might hang. We want them home, we want them to play, we want their time, and as children we accept no diplomats and enter no peace talks. Growing up I soon felt the insipid ache of insecurities seep in, pressures perpetuated by women, men, society, media. The Idea that your future will only be as golden as the ratio of 'beautiful' features on your face, the width of your waist or the wealth of your parents.

As a teenager, on some level I struggled to forgive my mum for doing the very best she could under impossible circumstances. I saw her as a victim of life, of society and of men, vowing I'd never find myself in such a situation. I set my mind to my passions: becoming a musician, writing, travelling and keeping a palm up like a bayonet in the face of any boy who might encroach on my sovereignty. This was my strength, as I saw it, and would ensure I hop-scotched passed the pitfalls that had ensnared the woman who raised me.

My bayonet and I managed to march through my early twenties with all the syncopated seriousness of a military parade in a banana republic. However, much like in the type of countries that hold military parades, the medals I so proudly wore on my chest were from battles I'd not yet fought. At 22 I was assaulted, by a man I've since realised had assaulted me almost every time I'd seen him previously.

I'd cut contact, to which he decided to break into my home, physically and sexually assault me. I won't include more detail. For plenty of you, that will be enough and I've more than relived it. However for some reading, they might wonder what kind of sexual assault? Had you spoken to him previously? What were you wearing? Rather than answer those questions, I would instead ask you, what are you trying to determine by asking them?

George Floyd was choked to death for 8 minutes and 46 seconds by a man whose job it was to protect him. Afterwards everyone agreed it was wrong; however some felt it necessary to highlight that George Floyd's behaviour in life was not spotless, as though that somehow warranted an impromptu death sentence without a trial, via knee to the neck while he begged for his life.

What does this have to do with womanhood? It represents what is, in my opinion, the greatest deficit in human compassion today and one that has plagued the progress of rights for all oppressed groups; that while most of the time we appear to share the same rights, our rights are not inalienable and are the first to be bartered, negotiated and traded when it becomes convenient to do so. Women's rights for so long existed only as an extension of men's property rights. Rapists were punished because of the shame they brought the victim's family, not the trauma it brought the victim.

Laws which allow rapists to walk free if they marry their victims still exist in countries today and existed in France up until 1994. While the silhouette of women's rights may look complete, its core is hollow and based on a falsehood. Women's struggle to turn their house of cards into a house of stone can seem pointless to those who only use it for its shade.

That night I believed I might die. Still, in the days after I convinced myself I had it together. In hindsight, this was like breathing a sigh of relief because a cobra's drawn its head back. The venom injected in my life that night was enough to let me limp on for a week or so before watching everything I'd once loved or enjoyed turn black, gangrenous and rot away. The following months revolved around violent flashbacks, panic attacks, paralytic nightmares and silent, drawn-out screams that would have Edvard Munch rolling in his grave to reach for a paintbrush. No happiness came from laughter with friends, no fulfilment from music, no rest from sleep. Not one sinew of my joy was left unmolested. My trusty bayonet revealed to be nothing but a daffodil.

It is impossible to cry at every news story and, as such, none of my friends could mourn for the old me for as long as I needed to mourn. Our sympathies lack the stamina of our misfortunes. It strikes me that I even wondered if I somehow deserved it. I felt ashamed and the tentacles of that age-old fallacy guided my own thinking. I reported a break in, damage to property and kept my mouth shut about the damage that had happened to me. I afforded more sanctity to the envelope of bricks and mortar than my own flesh and blood.

How did he feel so entitled to so much, and I to so little?

To me, that question is womanhood today. Acknowledging what we are entitled to, and what we deserve to be free from. Even today, 63% of all sexual assaults are not reported to police. And of those that are, a meagre 1.7% result in prosecution. Clearly, there's much to be done.

It is tempting to say that the slow steps I took to rebuild myself were worth it all but I don't think that's true. I think many women feel they have to say their trauma was worth it because it made them stronger or risk making the listener uncomfortable. But it doesn't need to be that way. My life would have been better if I was never assaulted. I don't have to be grateful for the strength it gave me. It's ok to wish the world was a little kinder instead. If that makes your listener uncomfortable, so be it.

Instead, I choose to be grateful for women like my mother and her mother, for doing an incredible job in the hardest of circumstances, despite self-entitled people treating them like expendable extras in their movie. I no longer see my mother's weakness, only her unfathomable strength in the face of adversity. I choose to be grateful for my friends. In the months I struggled to leave the house, my best friend posted a bar of Galaxy and a card that read 'you are stronger than you know, you will get through this'. That was a ray of light that blossomed into a dawn for me. Never underestimate the strength a kind word, a card or a simple smile can impart.

Womanhood is not defined by our body parts, our jobs, our femininity. It is abstract and for each of us to define ourselves. I consider it a lifelong journey, through which my experiences open my eyes to new ways of relating to, learning from, and empathising with women of the past, women of today, and those of our future.

I believe we each identify with womanhood in our own unique way and can draw strength from our existence as women to empower one another and collectively improve our world. I am privileged that from time to time I experience elements of this empowerment in my business, working on forward-thinking campaigns and with inspirational women from across the world, busy following their dreams and ambitions.

Womanhood is also about endeavouring to take responsibility for my life, own my pleasure, value my passions, trust my inner compass, stand up for myself and support - not compete with - other woman. I strongly believe we, as women, can empower men too, to rise above the stereotypes and walk beside us as equals. While my life has involved some terrible men, I am not and will never be "anti-men". This planet is packed with progressive, respectful, incredible men, my now husband being one.

I don't know whether the good fight is best fought with bayonets or daffodils. What I do know is women are closer to equality in society than they have ever been, but don't let anybody tell you that that's close enough.

Roxanne, 30

One Mystery Less to Know

Fingers
crooked with arthritis
brown spotted with age
parted the silky cream curtain
seduced by its satiny feel and
mysteries beyond

Come in
I have been waiting for your return

But, I just got here

No, you were here once before
I saw you

That wasn't me

Yes, it was.
Your hair was black, not silver
Your hands smooth and line free

No, that wasn't me

Yes. It was.
It was the day your daughter died
She was laid out on the bed
Resplendent in her white wedding gown
Designed only a year and a half before

You were kneeling beside her
Wishing with all your soul
That you could be dead, not her.
Your tears were silent
But your broken heart screamed like a wild banshee in the
night
Begging me to come for you
I came.
I saw you.

Yes, I whimper within the unleashed memory
That WAS me.
With confused creased brow
I ask
Why didn't you take me?

It was her time, not yours.
And, this time?

Only you can know that.
And, before that time is
Please learn to
Forgive yourself for all that you have not done
And have yet, to do.

That is all?

Yes, that is all.

The silky cream curtain slips from my fingers
Closing
Stepping back
Wisdom sighs in relief
One mystery less to know.

Pat , 71

Reflections

The first thing I ever wanted to be was a vet. Then an orchestral musician. Then a pharmacist. You might say I was undecided. In fact, in many ways, I still am. Growing up one thing was crystal clear: I was determined to work hard to support my future family and truly make a difference. This was largely driven by watching my father being able to provide for my mother, sisters and me.

He would bring sweets back from overseas business trips; spend evenings reviewing complex technical documents and even take me to his office to look around. I felt an immense sense of pride in what he did and looking back I feel fortunate to have had his support in pursuing a career in STEM.

When I expressed an interest in studying chemistry at university, my father organized a week of work experience for me with one of his contacts in a real-life working laboratory. (As an aside, in recent times I met the woman I worked for through a mutual musical friend. The world is so much smaller than it first appears).

Life is certainly never straightforward, and I am a firm believer that everything happens for a reason. My ending up moving home to finish my degree in order to look after my sisters and father following the sudden loss of my mum absolutely led me to being where I am today.

I joined the energy industry as a chemistry graduate following a clear path formed from my father's footsteps. Reasonably quickly I found myself taking on challenging leadership roles focused not only on broadening my knowledge but out of a self-created ideology that I had to somehow prove my worth not only to myself, but to all the men I worked both for and with.

About five years into my career, I took my first real risk and accepted an engineering role working on offshore oil platforms and rigs. As often the only woman in these harsh environments, I grew up quickly and learnt a lot about myself.

Spending two to three weeks at a time working nightshift with limited contact with the outside world certainly affects mental health and self-awareness. The fear of being seen as weak was real for me. A constant nagging feeling that I had something to prove was something that refused to leave my mind. To build a rapport with the crews I would laugh at their crass jokes, develop my vocabulary of filth to fit right in, and turn a blind eye to their derogatory ways of talking about the women in their lives. [I should add here this does not represent every man I worked with. In fact, a small minority. But they, perhaps inadvertently, had the biggest impact on me].

Reflecting on this time in my life I feel a deep sense of shame and regret. Shame for putting up with the behavior; regret for not making a concerted effort to improve the workplace for future generations. I altered my behavior, deviated from my values at times in an attempt to blend in and be seen (and treated) as equal to the men.

Of course, this was complete nonsense. I know that diversity of thought makes a team stronger and is vital to their success, so we should embrace and accept those differences. What is not often discussed or written about openly and honestly is how downright difficult it is to break down those barriers, not always putting our own self first: being selfless about the situation. This not only takes courage, confidence and a deep-rooted commitment to the cause, but it also takes time. For a while after leaving that role I detached myself from reality. Finding it easier to say 'I managed, so she can too' instead of being empathetic and supportive was, on reflection, an avoidance tactic I employed to ignore how I had reacted in those situations.

One thing I learnt from my time offshore is to be patient and not to be so hard on myself. Five years later I gratefully accepted my first senior role overseas and have grown into it ever since. Slowly but surely, I have found my voice and have been using it to advocate for and support other women at work.

To do this I have found that it takes mental strength to put my own ultra-competitive personality to one side, telling my inner voice that doing this for others in no way diminishes my own work or how I am perceived.

My father sadly passed away almost two years ago after battling a long cruel disease. Putting pen to paper to write this short story has helped me see a clear connection between experiencing the deep loss and my emotions. Since losing him I have felt a strong drive to carry on his legacy of supporting other women and so not only am I eternally grateful for my father's support when I was a child, but for fostering a deep sense of what equality means, feeling it running through my veins in everything I do.

It unfortunately remains common to be the only woman in the room at work. I reflect on these experiences coupled with fond memories growing up and know that my parents would both be so proud of where I am now. I am exactly where I am meant to be.

Alex, 34

Grow Through What You Go Through

We've all been there: you've recently split with your boyfriend and your self-esteem is almost non-existent. It happens.

Starting over, being vulnerable and pushing yourself out of your comfort zone after a relationship has ended is a daunting thought. Unfortunately, through my own experience, I've learned that us women are programmed entirely different from the male species. We are our own torturers; we must work through every emotion our brain can throw at us before seeing even a glimmer of light at the end of the tunnel.

But for any woman who feels like she isn't enough, for any woman who thinks that she will never love again - your feelings are normal, your feelings are valid. Give yourself a break, allow yourself to get experience each vital healing stage.

It's time to grow through what you go through. You are not alone.

The WORLD IS OVER Stage

The initial break up usually hits hard and you're probably finding it pretty hard to come to terms with the fact that you are a single lady once again. Thoughts and feelings at this brutally raw stage are usually around the same destructive theme of "why has this happened?" and "where did it all go so wrong?"

It's likely that you will spend the first few days moping around your house before attempting normal life again, barely throwing yourself together for work, but who cares, right? They should be grateful you have even graced them with your presence during this extremely difficult time.

You'll go to bed each night and indulge in your grief by selecting your most depressing break up playlist (we ALL have one) before sobbing into your pillow and waking up the next day looking like you've gone ten rounds in a boxing ring.

The I'M SINGLE AND I AM IRRESISTIBLE Stage

You're done being sad. You feel a rush of adrenaline and begin to feel like a strong, independent woman who doesn't need any man holding her back.

You're going to shave those legs and blow dry your hair better than any salon has ever done before and you're going to plaster that red lippy on like there is no tomorrow. There is no stopping you now.

You're going to go out tonight and disco winch any red-blooded male in sight, and why? Because you can and nobody is going to stop you.

That's the plan anyway. Behind the scenes, those nights usually consist of far too much alcohol, a lot of drunken tears, and if you do somehow manage to smooch anybody – it's probably going to be your best friend as you both cry into your kebabs at the end of the night in the taxi home.

The I WANT TO EAT MY OWN BODY WEIGHT Stage

So your last plan didn't work, but this one will. Food is your friend. Large pizzas are the only size you're ordering and if there's no chocolate in the cupboard for afters all hell is going to break loose.

Go for it ladies! If you want to eat, you eat! AND YOU EAT TILL YOU CAN'T EAT ANY MORE!

Your dressing gown is probably smothered in melted chocolate, and left overs for breakfast is better than no breakfast. That's progress.

The I MAY SERIOUSLY HURT YOU Stage

You're mad now, like really mad. Someone has hurt your feelings and it's not OK. A high alert should be broadcast to any ex-boyfriend who dares cross your path during this difficult time in your life.

How dare they hurt you? Who do these men think they are?

It's time to bite back. You are no delicate flower. You are a boss, the biggest, most fierce lion just waiting to pounce on the mention of his name. Your former other half could offer you a cup of tea right now and you would rather dehydrate than accept his gesture.

The WORLD IS OVER (PART 2) Stage

Ok, so you're not a lion; you're a fragile soul who just wants some understanding and some closure. You don't know what you're doing or how you will ever get through this wild emotional rollercoaster and the pain just feels bloody never-ending.

Suppressed feelings begin to resurface and they're just as raw as they were in stage one.

It's time to start from the top. Before you know it, the depressing play list has made a mighty comeback with brand new songs carefully selected to match your current feelings. You're drained. I get it, and it doesn't matter what anyone tells you – this will NOT "get better in time," and texting your ex is a perfectly good idea and will absolutely make things better. Won't it?

Spoiler: It doesn't.

The I'M GOING TO BE OK Stage

Wow. What is this feeling? You've woken up today and actually feel ... OK. Doing your make up today doesn't seem like such a chore anymore and, now that you come to think of it, you're actually looking quite bloody good even if you do say so yourself.

Yeah, you're single again, but so what? You have been for a while now and guess what? The world didn't stop turning. And that's not all, your inbox is on fire at the moment. You have options, you have new beginnings, new butterflies.

You've been through the war of your head and your heart, and guess what, you survived. It's time to prosper now as a new and improved woman.

As a woman, I know there will be so many others reading this who are sitting thinking "oh God, that's so me!" Well, AMEN sister, you are not alone. Break-ups suck, but they are inevitable and unfortunately if something isn't working or doesn't feel right, then I'm afraid as harsh as it may be, it has to disappear before something better is able to fill its space.

You made it. You always will.

Strong women grow through what they go through.

Paula, 30

Stronger

Being asked to write this piece is something that I was instantly passionate about because 'Womanhood' means a lot to me, and equally because the person that asked me is a very special lady in my life who deserves nothing more than my full and complete support. Although I jumped straight in, sat staring at my blank screen, it hit me that maybe I wasn't the right person for the job and that I didn't have a story anyone would be interested in hearing. So, I did what I usually do and decided to do a mind map of 'Womanhood', what this had meant for me in the past and present and where I stood with the word 'Empowerment'. I am 28 years old and still using the mind map technique I learnt in primary School, but it helped.

It helped me to look back on some of the key themes within my life and the experiences that made me who I am today. I am a very privileged person and by no means have I had a hard life in comparison to some, I know that I am incredibly lucky to have experienced some of the things I have, and be in the place that I am now. But nonetheless, I have also experienced some difficult times that have been traumatic, and those struggles themselves have led to struggles with my Mental Health.

At the age of 12 I lost my Mum and it felt like my whole world was turned upside down. Everything changed and everything felt scary. People still say to me now that they don't know how I coped with that, and the reality is that I didn't. I blocked it out as much as I possibly could and decided nobody could see the pain and everyone could only see that I was okay. As you would expect, my reluctance to deal with any grief or pain around losing my Mum had a significant impact on my Mental Health and eventually caught up with me. I replaced the pain of grief with the pain of anxiety and panic attacks, because although the intense panic attacks made me feel like I was dying, that pain was easier to deal with than the pain of losing the most important woman in my life.

As much as my Mum's parenting and love influenced who I am and moulded me into the person I am today, losing my Mum also moulded me and made me incredibly attuned to people's feelings. It made me empathetic, compassionate and constantly assessing and reflecting on my impact on others. I noticed people's pain before most would and I was careful in my thoughts and my words. For example, when I was younger every person I met assumed I lived with my Mum, so having to correct this or discuss this with complete strangers was often like a kick in the face. I am now so careful in the way that approach new people to avoid all assumptions and allow open conversations as I would hate to have anyone feel that way.

I feel it is important to approach people with empathy, never assuming I know what has led people to be in the places they are. I believe completely that everyone is trying their best with the situations they are in, and that often people that act unkindly or spitefully are dealing with the most horrendous pain. Another experience in my life which shaped who I am was when my seven year relationship, new home and engagement ended after my partner had a long term affair. Although I feel this incident itself hasn't defined who I am, it led to me feeling my lowest, having the least confidence I've ever had in myself and in a very vulnerable position. I had always avoided dealing with my pain and grief, because it just felt too much, but it was at this point I was encouraged by my friends and family to have counselling.

The counsellor I saw described herself as a feminist and was one of the most glamourous people I have ever met. I had no expectations about what counselling would be like, other than painful and depressing. What actually happened was this incredible lady gave me back myself and made my life feel colourful again. It was interesting to see that through our conversations how much of myself I had lost over the years and how much I would do anything I possibly could to help others, but expected absolutely nothing in return.

This focused partly on my relationship and particularly the impact of this on my Mental Health. I talked about how badly my ex-partner would react to my panic attacks and my fears. I explained how he would become very angry, would often leave me alone, would call me a 'freak' and told me that my behaviour had actually been what led him to cheat. My counsellor asked me to think of how I would respond if he had a panic attack, which of course was with love, reassurance, support and kindness. She then simply asked me why I would accept any less from the person I wanted to spend my whole life with.

It came down to me feeling I was such hard work that there would be nobody out there that had the patience to put up with me and that I was just not worth the stress. My counsellor recognised that I was in a vulnerable place and that my next relationship was very important, that if I wasn't able to recognise my worth, I would get into a relationship just as toxic, or worse. She told me to make a list of all the values that are important to me, the things that I wanted to see in the person I decided deserved to be my partner. I made a list which included kindness, empathy, humour, trust, respect, selfless-ness, a love of children, animals and family. I feel incredibly lucky and happy to say that I have found that person, and he is amazing and inspires me every day.

This counsellor who likely doesn't remember me has no idea how much she empowered me and how much she impacted my life. I can say today that I am a strong woman, because another strong woman opened my eyes to this. I am also lucky to have been surrounded by sisters and some amazing female friends who have given me their strength when I needed it, held my hand through the dark times and have celebrated with me through the highlights. I am aware a lot of women aren't this lucky, so it is important to me to be a champion for women and offer my support where I can.

Not only did this lady empower me to expect more from my relationships, I felt I finally had the strength to start dealing with my Mental Health and the grief I felt after losing my Mum. Since then I have seen another counsellor for my grief, had Cognitive Behavioural Therapy (CBT), Hypnotherapy, Acupuncture and Eye Movement Desensitisation and Reprocessing (EMDR) therapy. While this will be an ongoing process for me, I feel confident in myself that I can handle what is thrown at me and I feel happy with the person I have become. I feel passionate about empowering and supporting other women and throughout this experience I have got my degree which has enabled me to support women and families as part of my job.

It is a cliché, the saying that 'what doesn't kill you makes you stronger', but not only is it true, it shapes us into better, more considerate and more caring people. The grief of losing my Mum made me more compassionate and more empathetic of other people's struggles. The pain of anxiety and panic attacks made me more understanding and more passionate about people getting the care and help they deserve. The treatment I have had for my Mental Health, from my glamourous counsellor, made me feel strong and empowered. I use these skills I have developed every day in my job, and I have learnt that our struggles and pain can also be our strength. We are never alone in this, and every single day, every single small thing we do when life feels impossible, we should be proud of.

Amy, 28

Ode to Mommy – a Celebration of Womanhood

When I was young I always wanted to take in every stray animal, I couldn't bear the thought of any animal being abandoned. Most parents would have said "no way!" - especially one who was as allergic to pet hair as my mom was! However, she nearly always said yes because she also could not bear for an animal to be abandoned as she also loved animals as I did, and because she so loved me.

Then later I began to meet people and friends who had been abandoned and had no home. I would ask to bring them to our home. Again, most parents, especially a single parent with a small and full house of four children, would reasonably say something like "Sorry but we don' t have room." But mom nearly always made room, and would give them shelter and kindness, and without judgement. These friends thought of her as second mom throughout their lives. Through these acts of kindness and benevolence - which others might criticise her for - my mom taught me that life is more precious than any material thing; and that love and kindness to others, especially when they are most in need, rises high above any other human endeavour and brings us, in that moment, into the realm of true divinity.

This has defined who I am and/or who I strive to be as a woman, as a daughter, a sister, a friend, and mother. Borrowing the feminist phrase "the personal is the political," I feel the best way to honour and celebrate womanhood is through my personal lens of my mom, Joan, and how she has influenced my life and several others.

Joan, you could say, was a sort of "hands off" mom. She was definitely not what is now referred to as a "helicopter mom," always hovering waiting to save us from any dangers. Rather she would let us find our own way, and if/when we needed her she would be always be there. I remember her telling me something like "the more I trust you to be responsible, the more responsible you will be." As a result, we learned how to fall and how to get up on our own, and how to avoid falling again in the future.

Yet there were many times when we did need her to help us to get up, and not just when we were young but well into adulthood. We knew that our mom would always do anything she could to support us when we needed. In fact, she would happily go without to give to her children. However, we also learned to first try ourselves. This taught me to be as self-sufficient as possible, but also not to be afraid to ask for help if I need it. It also taught me to trust and believe in my own children to find their own way most of the time, and to also be ready and willing to support them when they needed throughout their adulthood – because let's face it, life is hard.

Joan also taught us about standing up for what is right. She faced great discrimination herself as a woman for having an interracial relationship, for having mixed race children, and for being a divorcee and single parent. However, this did not stop her from standing up for both her own and others' rights. My mom was active in the civil rights and women's movements in America in the 1960's and 70's. When she was married to my dad they had to buy a house they could barely afford because despite inter-racial marriages having recently been legalised no one would rent to a mixed race couple.

She worked so hard, so many late nights, such a work ethic, naively hoping this would be recognised and that she could break through that thick glass ceiling in her male dominated engineering firm. I remember her frustration as she watched her male colleagues - whom she trained up - get promoted and become her superiors, taking credit for her work. I remember how she was punished for remaining professional and avoiding the pigeonhole of "sex object" that she saw many of her female colleagues succumb to in order to survive or get ahead. I remember when she came home so angry when her boss called her in to his office for what she thought would be an acknowledgement of her tireless work on a successful project, only to tell her she was expected to wear pantyhose in the office – this was in the early 1980's.

I remember her teaching us that all of these things were wrong and discriminatory. I'll never forget when she quit this job of 18 years, suddenly and in a way which left her financially vulnerable, but nevertheless coming home with a broad smile and a look of enormous pride, saying "it was worth it just to see their faces when they realised they would have to do their own work!" She was confident she would land on her feet and she did. This taught me not to be afraid to take risks to do what is right for me.

It is true that we did not have a lot of material things as children as we did not have ample means, despite mom always working full-time and overtime. However, Joan gave me and my siblings something much more precious than toys and nice clothes. She gave us a sense of self belief and value, because of her unwavering belief in and value of us. As busy as she was, often working double shifts to support all of us, she would still take the time and interest to ask us about what we wanted to be or do when we grew up, and praised all of the qualities we had within us that would help us get there. She took an interest in our interests, in our hopes and in our feelings. We could never doubt her love for us. She also fostered our interest and curiosity in the world, taking us to beautiful places of nature, art, and philosophy. She taught us to be responsible, kind, respectful, accepting and non-judgmental toward others. These are the gifts she gave to us: priceless and enduring, and passed down to our children, and our children's children. There could be nothing of more value than this, and I am eternally grateful.

Allegera

A bus ride

I take a deep breath and step onto the night bus, present my pass and make my way down the aisle, my eyes scanning the few passengers on board. I take note of a man at the back of the bus with an unnerving expression watching me intently as I approach a seat. I tell myself it's probably nothing.

The intense neon light illuminating the aisle contrasts with the blackness of the night outside. Sat as close to the driver as possible, I glance out of the window to follow my journey home, but it's as dark as it gets in London and all I can see is my own grey-tinted reflection in the glass. Suddenly the engine roars as the bus gains speed, filling the eerie quietness of the night bus. I keep looking out the window for the whole journey until a robotic female voice announces that my stop is coming next, so I push the nearby bell and slowly stand.

Swivelling round, I make my way to the exit doors in the centre of the bus, looking up to assess the remaining passengers: just that man. He's looking down, scrolling on his phone no doubt. I take note of his clothes; a well worn black leather jacket. Nothing distinctive. I turn forward and face the double doors and am once again presented with my reflection, only I now can see him looking at me. Maybe he can sense my heightened nerves, my vulnerability. I could never fight off someone of that build. Perhaps he's thinking along the same lines?

I attempt to rationalise my thoughts; it's likely he's a normal guy returning home from work just like myself. He probably has a partner or even children waiting at home. My heart rate begins to increase, and my mind starts to recall an article I read years ago titled something along the lines of "things rapists look for in a victim." I attempt to recall the entire list, and one particular statement comes to my mind suggesting that rapists target women with their hair tied up as it makes them easier to grab from behind. Without realising, my hand is already traveling to the top of my head and my fingers feel the tightly secured bun I prepared this morning for work.

As I try to get through the few long seconds remaining on the bus, I calculate the walk from the bus stop to my front door; if I walk fast I can get there sooner, but the road is long, narrow and residential so there's more chance of an encounter with a stranger. The alternative is down a narrow flight of concrete stairs which lead straight to my road and then roughly 20 steps to my front door. I automatically start to imagine approaching the stairs to find a male figure in the darkness at the bottom, waiting patiently for victims. My heart beats even faster, and I question why I continue to commit to these late night shifts..

At last the bus stops and the doors open. The cold air hits bluntly, but after enduring the stale, clammy atmosphere of the bus it feels refreshing. I step off with pace and shoot a quick glance behind me; the man is stepping off as well. He raises his head and notices me looking. Panic hits. I hastily make the decision to take the stairs and speed down the road, conscious of trying not to show how afraid I am. I look behind and he seems to be following me. Where is he going? Does he live around here? I stare straight ahead and can now see the top of the stairs. I look around again. Parked cars and typical town houses. I search around, desperate for someone else to appear but there's only him. All I can hear are his footsteps. Is he trying to catch up with me? Finally reaching the stairs, I hurtle down with such speed that I can feel the strain on my ankles as I land heavily at the bottom.

Finally my front door is in sight and I think I've lost him but I'm not there yet. My walk turns to a run, and I reach the front door. Key in. One last look around. Enter the house. Slam shut the door, lock it and breathe. A flood of relief washes over, with an unjustified wave of achievement followed by feeling so stupid.

Holly, 28

Mum Gut

I'll be honest: having children wasn't always part of the life plan. To be frank, I had previously felt indifferent about marriage and children and whilst I wasn't sure what I wanted for my future, it certainly wasn't this. I met my now husband at 18 years old on the bar scene. We both enjoyed a drink, loved to dance and we were highly compatible in all the ways that really count. Fast forward to now; we are happily married with two beautiful children.

As someone who didn't ever identify as 'the mum type' I was surprised to find something switch very early in my 20's when I felt quite certain a family was what I wanted. But even at this stage in my life I think I imagined Motherhood as just part of my life. I certainly wasn't going to be consumed by it. I would still be career driven, highly motivated to do 'something' with my life - kids wasn't going to be just it, not for me.

When I first held my daughter in my arms after a difficult and taxing pregnancy, my world was shaken. What I thought I knew about myself was instantly lost and I was swept up in a whirlwind of undying love I never dreamed I could feel. Maybe this was IT after all. Don't get me wrong; I still have other ambitions, dreams, passions and interests that extend beyond my children, but my children motivate me in a way I could never have foreseen. Suddenly I wanted to be the best mother I could be and that felt like the most important job in the world. And that big world? Suddenly I wanted to change it.

I was initially surprised at how entirely natural Motherhood felt to me. As someone who never had younger siblings and had altogether no experience with babies, I was as surprised as anyone to find myself instantly in love and sure of myself in recognising her needs, and more comfortable providing for her, than I thought possible. It was about 3 months in when my love and caffeine fueled bubble first got popped.

I was visited by a good friend who mid conversation brought up the dreaded conversation of sleep:

"How's the sleep going?"

"Well, there isn't much of it going on to tell you the truth"

The truth was she was feeding constantly; she hadn't really worked out day and night yet; and I wasn't getting much sleep.

Ironically, I was ok with it but my friend's next words stung.

"If you keep feeding her and going to her she will never sleep; it sucks but you can't go to them every single time they whine"

This got me. Had I been doing it all wrong after all? Would my baby really NEVER sleep? Was I creating issues further down the line?

Panic set it and after frantic goggling we decided to try sleep training. It felt totally unnatural to me but still I persevered. After all, this is what parenting was, right? Making tough choices?

After a dreadful night and lots of tears from both of us I decided I never wanted to put us through it again and the truth is I never did. Following this my daughter remained a terrible sleeper until about two. Time and time again I would struggle with thoughts of self-doubt and time and time again I was bombarded with unwanted and unhelpful advice. The truth was, my 'Mum' gut was telling me my babies sense of security was important and I didn't have to or want to let my baby cry, and I was fighting to drown out other unwanted noise and criticism.

Sleep wasn't the only parenting issue. I faced criticism and each unintentional comment or piece of unwanted advice only made me feel more and more incapable as a Mother. I often had people remark at how 'together' I was or how 'easy' I made it look when the truth is I often felt entirely incapable of the very thing that meant the most to me.

Luckily, my journey was a positive one. I learned over time to ignore any unwanted criticism and only accept advice that supported my parenting ethos. Along with this I surrounded myself with a tribe of women who shared similar views on parenting and their support has been invaluable.

With information overload, contrasting parenting advice readily available, and a society that is far too comfortable with criticising women in general, it is no wonder that I and so many others have struggled with self-doubt. I encourage women to listen to their 'Mum gut' and have faith in their chosen methods because you know your babies better than anyone. Accepting my mistakes, surrounding myself with love and ignoring negativity has allowed me to be a more confident, perfectly imperfect, but self-assured parent. I am now a proud Mother of two amazing children. I can look at my cheeky six-month-old and my confident, fierce, intelligent, dramatic, secure and wildly affectionate three-year-old daughter with pride, in the knowledge that they grew from my love and I will continue to grow from theirs every single day.

God is woman

She is Love.
How vast, how wide, how deep is your Love?
Unending, unconditional; it is from your love that I came into being.
Fill me up and refresh me.
Because of Her I overflow with a love that will never run dry.
A love that is impossible to grow old, impossible to be stagnant.
Her love leads and guides.
She's a radical love that, once tasted, your days will forever be different, all eyes and hearts captured in awe and wonder.
To be clothed in Her love is to be soft,
yet strong, courageous, resilient, attuned and attentive.
I rest in Her Love.
She is Maker.
Unapologetic about the work of Her hands.
Creation shows glimpses of who she is.
Earth tamer, ocean pourer, hill dresser, mountain maker;
yet she knows me, hears me, sees me.
Freedom is found as I sit and marvel at Her.
She causes me to dance through the wildest of days, through the darkest of nights, inviting the moody clouds of change to sway my way;
I know that with Her, anything is possible.
I am Her creation.
She is Peace.
It's the silver lining to every earthly day,
the peace that transcends my understanding,
that injects me with hope
and tames the wild winds that often attempt to sweep me up.
I'm infected with Her peace.
I'll dot it through the cafes, drop it in the streets and paint my family red with it.
Her peace is my anchor.
She is Home.
Engulfed in Her warm arms, my face pressed against Her chest;
Her heartbeat is my rhyme, the very reason I choose to fully live.

She welcomes The Joneses and homeless alike,
Her door always open with the kettle on,
waiting, ever patient, for all to come;
to sit and to simply be.
She is my source.
She is Woman.
Her kindness is unending.
She fights our battles, fights for justice; Her wisdom will tell me
when to be still.
She enables and celebrates all.
She listens to and welcomes all.
She is present, she is active, she is still.
She is all things good.
She is all things true.
She is all things beautiful.

Elle, 32

The power of music

I'd never really been a person that music affected emotionally when growing up. That doesn't mean I don't appreciate music, but I was very rarely moved to tears when listening.

From my teenage years, I grew up on a musical diet of Black Sabbath, Pink Floyd, Led Zeppelin, Jethro Tull, David Bowie and Yes, amongst many others. Latterly, during my three sons' teenage years, I was introduced to Metallica, Killswitch Engage, Avenged Sevenfold and Disturbed during the times that the Sky TV music channel 'Kerrang' was permanently on (or so it seemed!) when they were at home.

The energy of that music uplifted my soul, the slower pace of love songs or ballads couldn't compete as far as I was concerned.

All that changed in October 2011 however.

Imagine having to watch your son go through the worst year of their life and being unable to do a damn thing but support them through it.

As a mother, it's unbearable.

We're the human incubators that nurture our children inside our bodies until they're ready to be born, we feed them with the milk our bodies produce, care for them and make them better when they get ill, hold them tight when they are sad or hurting, listen to them when they're worried and reassure them throughout the many stages of their lives.

We're not supposed to hand one of them over to complete strangers because there's no other choice and hope, oh how we hope, that they can save their life.
Cancer.

Cancer did that.

Cancer took away my belief that I could always make my child better and removed my right to keep my child safe.

Rob, at the age of 23 years old, was diagnosed with germ cell cancer in January 2011, with a mediastinal tumour insidiously growing uninvitedly and unknowingly within his chest cavity.

From that point on, Rob was not only our middle son, brother of Ad and Toby, nephew, cousin and friend, he was also a cancer patient going through intense bouts of chemotherapy treatments at St Bartholomew's Hospital in London.

During these sessions that lasted for ten months in total, which resulted in inevitable side effects of sickness, diarrhoea, nosebleeds, high fevers and extreme fatigue to name but a few, Rob would remove himself from the harsh and relentless reality that he'd been thrown into by the simple process of putting his earplugs in, allowing the heavy metal bands he adored into his head to entice him into an alternative world of grunts, groans, riffs and complicated heavy drum beats, so that he could block out all the bad stuff.

Rob's constant music companions were American Head Charge, Down, All That Remains, Machine Head and System of a Down predominantly, who helped to keep a semblance of normality when outside physical influences and internal mental turbulence threatened daily to overwhelm him.

Although that music genre can sound aggressive and harsh, a sense of calmness descended upon him when he was unable to verbalise his frustrations or escape from the 'antsy' periods after a chemo session had finished and the neutropenic stage started; a period when he was waiting for his white blood counts to rise and he'd finally begin to feel well enough to be allowed home.

The power of music = The power of solace.

Being an enthusiastic drummer himself, in a heavy metal band when he was a teenager that had played gigs in several local venues, meant that his fingers were constantly tapping along to the music in his head wherever he was, even at the dinner table.

I'd love to say that he still plays the drums enthusiastically and that he still appreciates listening to those bands.
I'd love to…. but I can't.

In October 2011, at a follow up appointment after a chemo session, Rob was given the awful news that nothing more could be done for him as the secondary leukemia, that developed during the summer and failed to respond to a transplant of stem cells donated by his older brother Ad, was too aggressive to be halted. Subsequent investigation into other clinical trials proved fruitless and therefore he was entering the palliative phase of the remainder of his life.

Rob, the bravest person in that room, wanted to know how he would die.

His Doctor, an incredibly empathetic man, took a deep breath and being as honest as he could without being too graphic, informed him that what would probably happen was that he would get increasingly fatigued as his blood got thicker, eventually exhausting his heart as it tried to pump it round his body, therefore it might just happen that he'd go to sleep one night and not wake up, without pain if that was what he was worried about.

On that last car journey home from St Bart's, Rob had obviously been pondering upon the information he was given and asked if I would sleep in his bedroom with him as he didn't want to be alone if that happened.

I had no hesitation in reassuring him that I would do just that and would make up a bed on the floor from that night onwards. Rob nodded, turned round in his seat and placed his earplugs back in, taking comfort once more in losing himself within the vibrant music that had supported him throughout that year.

Thus began our nightly routine as soon as Rob got settled into a comfortable position in his bed. I'd lightly massage his hands first, using my own instinctive form of hand reflexology that had helped to calm him during his chemo sessions, then I'd move onto stroking his forehead gently and gradually work my way over the rest of his head to finish on his ears.

If I close my eyes I can still feel the texture of his hands and head to my touch, his skin having a dry warmth to it due to the chemo leaving it parched. I can remember the stubbly sensation of his head as his hair struggled to regrow, with the bumpiness of the many moles and childhood chickenpox scars standing proud under the gentle touch of my fingers.

By this time his sleeping tablets had kicked in and combined with the massage, he was ready to turn over onto his side, hug his pillow and start to gently breathe deeper as he fell into, hopefully, a comfortable night's sleep. Then I could begin a Reiki healing on him.

When I'd finished, I would stand next to him in total silence, listening to his breathing, watching his chest rise and fall, gazing at his handsome face with his beautifully shaped eyebrows and closed eyelids no longer framed by long sweeping eyelashes that any female would envy.

I willed myself to remember every single detail, filled with dread at the thought of losing him but thankful, for that moment at least, I still had him in front of me. I refused to let myself cry when watching as I didn't want to wake him.

I needed to be strong for his final months, weeks, days perhaps. Who knew? I wouldn't let his last memories of me be tainted by hopeless tears…

Practicalities had to be adhered to however. My food cupboards needed stocking up so one morning after giving Rob his meds and leaving Ad in charge, I started the short drive into Colchester to Tesco's.

I hadn't gone far when a song started playing on the car radio.

'I don't want to miss a thing' by Aerosmith.

I'd heard it many times before but for the first time ever as I listened to the lyrics, they grabbed hold of my heart and squeezed until I was hurting. They hit me so hard I had to pull over to the roadside as I was blinded by tears.

From the very first line, I knew that I would never be able to listen to that song again without breaking down as the words were so relevant.

'I could stay awake just to hear you breathing
Watch you smile while you were sleeping
While you're far away and dreaming
I could spend my life in this sweet surrender
I could stay lost in this moment forever
Every moment spent with you is a moment to treasure'

When Steven Tyler reached the line 'And I don't want to miss a thing', I couldn't stop sobbing as I realized that this was exactly what I was doing every single night.

It was torture but I continued listening as I needed this emotional outpour to happen because I wouldn't do it in front of Rob. Granted that the song is from a lover's point of view, however each line was shredding my heart as it continued to verbalize my desperate emotions –

'I just want to hold you close
I feel your heart so close to mine
And just stay here in this moment
For the rest of time…'

The power of music = The power of love.

Rob died in St Helena's Hospice in Colchester at 3.45pm on Saturday 10th December 2011 with his family surrounding his bedside.

He never knew the effect that song had on me because I didn't tell him. I would have broken down and it wasn't the time to do that.

Music can restore a cherished memory at will, take us back to a place of happiness and laughter, equally to a place of loneliness, teenage angst – you name it, there's a song or lyric that will fill that space adequately to help, as music is at the core of many, if not all, of us.

In my case, music was finally giving me permission during 2011 to let my pent-up emotions have an overdue outpouring when I was alone, with no-one trying to comfort me or help to stop the flow and I was so grateful, because that was my time.

Now it's my 'go to' song when I need to have an emotional release, proving to me that the equation is simple.

The power of music can equal the power of solace resulting in the power of never-ending love.

Lorna, 62

About me

I am a hamster on a wheel of cooking, cleaning, washing.
I am a Forth Bridge of phoning, caring, worrying.
I am a closed book of mistaken loving.
I am a candle of hope that it will be alright in the end.

Gill

Different from my Mother

For as long as I can remember I've desperately wanted to tread a different path from my mother. Maybe not aged three, when I followed my mother around as she pushed her Bex Bissel carpet sweeper singing 'Que Serra Serra, whatever will be will be', to Doris Day on the radio. In the picture in my mind she is wearing late fifties, full skirt and apron.She was singing to me and my father was absent. I was told he lived and worked in London during the week. My mother may have struggled, but to me, it felt blissfully happy.
My little granddaughter, now at the same age, only has two settings. Sad can be dramatic and intense, but is usually short lived. She can easily be reset to 'happy' with a lolly.
If only life stayed this simple.

I think it started with the grinding sickness I felt in my stomach as I lay awake listening to the voices of my mother and father getting louder. Then the dread of the first bang or crash. I imagined my mother's head splitting as it hit the wall. Myself on the top bunk, my little brother below. We planned our intervention. Decided who would face the anger of our father. It was usually down to me to go. My older brother's room was further away. As the eldest he would have been at more risk from my father.

Even though my father threw the punches, I blamed her. I observed the lead up, sensed the danger, and knew the pattern. I focused on my mother's role in the dangerous tango. From our bedroom I willed our mother to stay silent, nod in agreement, to flatter or calm our father. I felt it was within her power to appease and contain him. By six I couldn't understand how my mother hadn't learnt the rules I knew so well.

His children all saw him as unpredictable, moody, dangerous. Knowing what he was like, why did she speak back to him, disagree, provoke him? I learnt to view my father as a human landmine to tiptoe around so as not to detonate him.I thought I would be different. Be able to survive better than her. It was all about adapting your behaviour to manage his.

The responsibility weighed heavily. If I drifted off to sleep whilst they argued, I would wake with a start thinking that I should have kept alert, ready to protect her. My mother would say, 'one day I'll just pack up and leave you all'. The prospect of being left with my father was the worst scenario I could ever imagine. I didn't think I could protect us and care for everyone. She never did leave us, or our father.

I could never understand why she stayed in a marriage which made her so unhappy. She would never say anything disloyal to him. She would make excuses and put his temperament down to various worries...Perhaps she just loved him? I made up my mind early to never marry or depend on a man. And certainly, to never end up with anyone like my father.

The older I became, the more critical I was of my mother as she put up with my father's behaviour and constant affairs. Sometimes under her nose with teenage lodgers barely older than myself. I blamed her, not him, when he left us in the holidays to volunteer at archaeological digs. I assumed the attraction would be the young female volunteers. My mother remained in denial throughout.

Watching my father constantly putting my mother down, meant that I too developed little respect for her, and blamed her for putting up with a life with him. I fantasised constantly about leaving home and finally managed to. At seventeen I found the insecurity and discomfort of a room in a squat preferable to remaining with my family.

Despite my intentions I found I was desperate for recognition from men. I moved even further from my goal of independence to end up homeless, as the relationships broke down.

I set the bar very low and generally they met it. I wasn't expecting to rely on them financially or emotionally and would walk off when they cheated. I thought of men like baby birds, you took into your nest, where you would feed and preen them. Then they waddled off into someone else's nest.

In spite of my disastrous love life, I managed to work and gained O levels and then A levels through part time college courses. At twenty-three, I became a mature student at University. Expecting my father to be proud of me, his only remark was, 'don't believe everything they tell you'.

In those six years I had crystallised my opinion about men. My politics were unforgiving, and I even toyed with the idea of separatism. If I hadn't continued to fancy men, I might have become a lesbian separatist feminist as I equated men with oppression. This was not meant to be.

After my first year at university, I got pregnant. The father, by then, had left the area for employment. I took a year off, and returned the second year with a seven-month old daughter. Through the campus nursery, I met many other single mothers who became a strong and supportive circle of friends. We definitely weren't victims. Most of these women, had made conscious decisions to live without male support. I embodied a political statement. At twenty-five, I had refused the offer of marriage from my daughter's father. I also sent another boyfriend packing, when he wanted to become a substitute father for my daughter.

When my daughter was three, maybe tired of the struggle of coping alone, I met someone twice my age. He offered me financial security and was also nice to me. I temporarily lapped up the comfort, but it was short lived. Like all of my relationships, thus far, I could not make the commitment .I couldn't risk ending up like my mother.

Yet he was kind and caring, and actually nothing like my father. Inevitably, I followed what was becoming a pattern and swapped him for someone who was moody, difficult, and cheated on me. I just didn't seem as attracted to men who were kind.

As I left university and started a long career within Probation, I rigidly held on to my independence. I brought my own house, had my own income, so I wouldn't depend on anyone else.

Life with my moody and difficult boyfriend, continued to feel like a roller coaster. We didn't discuss the future or make a commitment. Maybe I needed the drama of arguments and reconciliation to maintain an edge to the relationship? But it was exhausting and not a great environment for my daughter.

Eventually my boyfriend left to marry the woman he had been two timing me with. I was devastated, even though I made it clear this wasn't what I wanted. On the rebound, I decided I also needed marriage and security. I chose someone who had a poor history of relationships and also had a habit of walking out of employment. Much of our time together consisted of me finding him work, only to have him walk out for fairly minor reasons. He had one failed marriage under his belt and a daughter who became my long-term stepdaughter.

Two years in and our marriage was in tatters. He packed the few things he had arrived with, and left. Luckily, I still had my house, my own income, and we had another daughter.
I followed up with a brief physically abusive relationship, and then a noncommittal, ten year one. After numerous break ups it eventually fizzled out. It dawned on me that I had preferred to invest in relationships which were doomed to failure.

In some ways it was not so different from my mother's experience? Dissimilar only in terms of numbers.
Don't get me wrong -all of my previous partners had positive things about them which made me fall in love with them, but they also had clear warning signs, written in bold, which I ignored.

At the age of 57, I finally met and married someone different from my usual pattern. Whatever the difficulties in the relationship, it makes up for in closeness and commitment. Between us we have eight grandchildren, and eight years later, it's my longest consistent relationship.

I now recognise the strength it took for my mother to endure a controlling abusive relationship, whilst managing a successful career, and caring for three children,the best she could.

Age has given me perspective and allowed me to forgive her for her choices, as I hope my daughters will forgive me, mine. I am grateful to have inherited some of her strength and drive, and were she still alive I would finally let her know the good things I have inherited from her.

To my daughters, and in memory of my mother Beatrice.

Penny, 65

Sarah's Story (Part Two)

You make me laugh you lot, with your talk of glass ceilings and sexual harassment. You should have had my life. Started out well enough. I was the only girl with two older half- brothers and little Joe, as well as my Da of course. Called me their bonny lass and nothing was too good for me. No going out to work, just helping Mam about the house. And then, I met Robson. The lads warned me he was a bit of a hot head- didn't care for the bosses, had ideas. But there was something about him and of course I couldn't say "no".

I fell pregnant and he wasn't too pleased- not part of his plan, he said. Took a lot of persuading, well maybe more than talk- but he did marry me in the end, just eight weeks before Lizzie was born. And we got on well enough for a couple of years but he was always on about changing the world. To tell you the truth, I didn't always listen. His family were great talkers. Then George was born and Robson got caught damaging the machinery in the pit. Up in court. Not that he saw it as a disgrace. Liked to think that he was a martyr, fighting the system. Fined six shillings. But the fine wasn't the worst part- his family rallied round- he had a large family. No, the worst part was he couldn't get work: blacklisted. So then he decides, we'd go to America. Never thought about what that meant for me, leaving Mam, Da and the lads.

We went from Liverpool, got to New York on April 1st.1869. Don't ask me about the voyage, steerage with two small bairns! I didn't take much note of New York, I was just so miserable and Robson was so excited. We were off to Ohio, to a place called Liberty Township in Trumbull County. He saw it as the promised land. And to be fair, so did a lot of other people from all over the world. There were days when I couldn't find anyone to talk to because there were so many languages there, And not much liberty either.

Coal had been discovered on this farmer's land and he was making a fortune out of men like Robson and all the other fools. He didn't pay them in real money, just tickets to spend in his shops. It was a lot worse than back in County Durham and as for the living conditions… But one thing I had learned about Robson was that he never liked to admit that he might have made a mistake. He used to get angry with me when I was miserable, missing Mam and all the people I knew and when I said it was a case of out of the frying pan and into the fire he said I was hysterical and didn't know what I was talking about.

I'm not quite sure what happened next but I ended up in the West Virginia Asylum. They said I was lucky because it was the best place to be. Anyway they let me out after 8 months and it was back to the same old place. Robson seemed pleased to have me back and Sarah was born in January 1873.

After that we came home to Tow Law - don't ask me how - Robson saw to all that. My little Ruth was born - I named her after my Mam. Two and a half years between those girls and two continents. Then there was Tom and Joe and John Eddie. But we were on the move again, to Yorkshire this time. We had to leave little Ruth behind with her Uncle Joe. The family said it was for the best. As usual, nobody asked me what I thought. Ruth was never strong like the others and she died the year before Henry was born. By that time we were back in Durham. Mam died at the beginning of 1887, just a couple of months after little Mabel, my last, was born in November.

I did find it a struggle, Robson always busy with his union affairs and nobody taking me seriously. I couldn't read and write like some of them but that didn't mean I was stupid. And if I did get upset, they never listened to my problems. "That's Sarah for you. That's the way she is. Take no notice." But it got worse and I did do some silly things. I went out in the street in my nightdress and I did get cross with one of the girls and threatened her with a poker.

I felt it was all getting too much for me and I had no one to turn to, now that Mam and Da were dead and the lads no longer around. I did have one good neighbour but I couldn't always rely on her. There was only Robson and his family and they never liked me. One day they sent for the police and had me committed to the asylum. Robson never lifted a finger in my defence, left it all to his sister. Mind you, the Durham Miners paid the fees, out of respect for him I suppose. He died three months after I went in and they kept on paying for the next 38 years.

Of course, I didn't take it lying down, I argued that they should let me out and I worried about the children. I even tried to escape by breaking windows with a broom handle! When I argued, they said I was hysterical: when I was confused, they said I was losing my grip on reality: when I mentioned places in America, they laughed and shook their heads: when I clung to one of them hoping for comfort, they shuddered and shook me off.

They said I looked demented; that I neglected myself, was slovenly and untidy. Over and over again, they said I was uncooperative and making no effort to get well though they never suggested how I might do this or how they might help me. And they wrote all this down in their ledgers. They liked it best when I sat quietly knitting or when I swept the floors or helped them give out the food.

They even sent me to the other end of the country to Fisherton Asylum in Salisbury for a few years and they said they thought I was much improved when I came back but not enough to leave obviously.

I was 40 when I went in and 78 when I died. My children were parcelled out to various members of Robson's family; they grew up without me. They married and had children, my grandchildren whom I never saw. I remember Tom coming with his wife once. He was 10 when I went in and he and Mabel, the youngest, grew up together.

Tom was down the mine before he was 12 so I suppose his wages helped to support Mabel. He and Lizzie had been married a while when they came to visit and she was in the family way. I hoped she'd be luckier with him than I was with Robson. Mind you, I could see his father in him: wanted to change the world, never mind what it cost his family. But I was told that he sent money to one of the doctors to buy me extra comforts though I don't recall seeing either the doctor or the comforts, or for that matter him again. Too busy saving the world. I did hear he went to prison in the War. Didn't believe in killing. Left Lizzie to face the insults and to find means to keep their seven bairns fed and clothed. His Da all over again.

In the end, I got used to it, I suppose. I was born at the wrong time. I had no education. The men in my life made all the decisions. My Da and the lads, Robson, the policemen who came and called the doctor who certified me, all the doctors in all the asylums. They decided and I suffered the consequences.

My "madness" was all my fault; I could get better if I tried. I even had the stupidity to suffer from Diabetes before they knew how to treat it.

I don't know what you would have of made of my life. Now, if I had had yours…

Sarah Bell nee Young 1847-1926.

Beth, 86

<u>"It's just a blip"</u>

Maybe I should start by saying this. I was never really the sort of girl who dreamed of getting married. It's a family joke that I always said I didn't want to get married because I didn't want to "wash their smelly socks!" (I was always very wise...)

By the time I got to about 26, I realised that I was OK on my own. I had amazing friends and family, two beautiful nephews and I would rather be on my own than be let down by a partner.

Then Simon popped back in to my life. We had been together years before but it had all gone slightly awry and, after the "best friends falling in love" ended poorly, I decided that if I was to be on my own, then that was just fine. But deep down I always knew there would never be another Simon.

Anyway, fast-forward a few years and there we were, saying "I do" in front of our friends and family. Dreamy wedding, beautiful honeymoon in the Cotswolds and, bam, I was pregnant. How perfect is that? Honeymoon baby, no troubles in falling pregnant, we were living the dream. Still not 100% sure about the whole Motherhood thing, I felt a real mix of emotions.

The first 10 weeks I suffered badly with morning sickness. (All day everyday sickness) But then my symptoms started to subside and I was feeling normal again. I felt so relieved as I could start to function.

Eleven weeks exactly, I went to the toilet in the morning and I had started to bleed. The absolute fear and panic is still palpable, even just writing the words down. Simon was away on exercise, which also unfortunately made him pretty much uncontactable. I called my sister and the doctors and I had an examination. The Doctor said she couldn't be sure as my cervix was still closed, but she would book me in for a scan. After 24 hours of pretty much just panic and heartbreak, I went for my scan.

I waited at the hospital, sitting with other expectant Mums and was called in. At this point, I have to recognise our sonographer. She was called Sam. She was- without a doubt- one of the kindest, most supportive medical practitioners I have ever met. She informed me I had suffered a missed miscarriage. No baby anymore. Just a pregnancy sack. No real way of knowing when this had happened, she guesstimated around 7 weeks. What? What even was that? I had never heard of this before, neither had my sister, who has two boys.

The rest is just a blur. I left the room with a folded up leaflet and no baby. As I got outside, a woman was being wheeled through with her new born. I got caught between the bed and the wall and had to watch this blissfully happy woman with her baby, whilst my world had literally just stopped moving.

Telling Simon was one of the worst experiences of my life. He was incredible. Simon's only concern was that I was OK and that I didn't blame myself. But, when this happens how can you NOT blame yourself? He had his own emotions and feelings but I think he just took on the role of protecting and looking after me.

Physically, the miscarriage took three weeks to fully complete. Again, I just thought you "had a miscarriage." And it ended. I chose to let things happen naturally. I didn't realise it would be three weeks of scans, appointment and then sadly enough, medical intervention anyway. Mentally, I didn't realise you could grieve so much for someone you hadn't even met.

When I first came home, I remember feeling like I wanted to disappear. Just 'poof!' Snap my fingers and I would be gone and no one would feel this horrific pain and grief I had inflicted, in them. Not suicidal, but just be gone and I wouldn't have to deal with any of it.

I was very lucky to have such an amazing support network. My sister is my rock, so between her, Simon and my close friends and family, I knew we would be ok. I know not everyone has this, so I was, and still am, so appreciative.

People really tried to do and say the right things and most did. I also realised that, people say random things, like a Filofax of inappropriate things to say. But honestly, it all comes from a good place. Here are few "favourites..."

"It's just a blip"
"Well, at least you didn't get to 12 weeks"
"It's great now you know you can get pregnant"
"It could be so much worse though, Gem"
"So sorry I can't come and sit with you, I've just realised I've got yoga."

Of course, you get people who don't step up at all. But, I think this made me re-evaluate who we needed to carry on with and who we could put to the side. So surely this is a positive.

One thing I found extremely hard was that, I couldn't find an honest, brutal account of miscarriage. The physical and emotional pain. That blew my mind. Most things are wrapped up in quotes and positivity, and of course the time comes when you may need that. So I will always be honest if anyone asks, so they don't feel alone and they know another woman's real, no holds barred experience. Then to let them know it does get a little easier with time.

We decided to try again. We were advised to wait a month just so the pregnancies didn't interfere with each other and again, I fell straightaway. But this time felt so different. Taking the test made me feel dizzy. I wanted a baby so much, but I couldn't even contemplate another life changing loss.

I felt like I had no emotional connection before 12 weeks and would often think I would not relax until the baby was here: I don't think I really did. At 20 weeks it was discovered that our baby had a kidney disorder, inherited from me. Was this my fault we lost our first baby? A whole new set of unexplained questions started rolling around in my head.

We were lucky enough to see "Sam the sonographer" on our early scan with the second baby. It was poetic that she has seen us go full circle and I am forever grateful for her.

Simon and I have since done everything we can to raise awareness and fundraise for the miscarriage association. I am now a media volunteer too. They kept me going, especially on the long sleepless nights of pregnancy number 2.

I personally don't feel there is enough support for women who have gone through a miscarriage and we are left to simply process it and move on. Even my midwife messaged and said, "So sorry Gemma. Hugs."

This is not the most cheery of pieces. But I think it's important that even if one woman reads this and it resonates with them, then our story will make a little more sense.

Once you speak to people about your experience, you would not believe how many stories you hear of "that happened to me, my Sister, my Mum." It's just crazy. So, when Alex asked me to write for this amazing collection of stories, I jumped at the chance. People whisper miscarriage, like it's a dirty word. Stiff upper lip, we don't talk about it. So this brings zero awareness.

If this has happened to you, talk about it. For as long as it takes. There's no time limit on grieving. People will stop asking, but make sure you do what you need to do, no matter how uncomfortable it may make others. There are an abundance of women all in this secret little club; with our inboxes open and our shoulders ready to cry on.

After all of this, I must say I'd do it all again in a heartbeat. The second pregnancy was very different, but I really did appreciate it so much more and every day was a day close to meeting our baby.

We now have our Beatrice. She's four and the best little human I've ever come across - I may be being biased. She is funny and tough and fiery and the most caring little girl I could wish for. But I will always remember our little first baby and wonder who they could have been.

Gemma, 36

<u>You</u>

You plague my dreams,
My relationships,
My friendships,
My ability to love and be loved.

You are in the shadows,
Lurking,
Always there.
Your touch still felt,
Your sweat still smelt,
It burns.

The hurt inflicted,
Still real,
Imprinted in my mind.
The scars still there,
Haunting,
Taunting.

In the backdrop,
Shading all that is joyful,
Watching,
Waiting,
Unable to escape.

The name that cannot be spoken.
The shame devouring,
Agonizing,
All encompassing.

I long for the end,
For your death.
Would that release me from your grip?
Your torment?
This anguish?

Strong, empowered feminist,
Ha!
Yet I cannot say your name,
Put words to this pain,
Speak of what you did.

I am fraudulent.
Helping others,
Pushing others,
Never to push myself.

Practice what you preach they say,
But how?
You are so potent,
If I let you out you will devour.

Fuck it!
Take another pill,
Down another drink,
Seep into the abyss,
Where your name does not exist.

Charlotte,33

Female fronted is NOT a genre

"People have literally looked me in the eye and said that I'm not a musician. They've looked me in the eye and told me that I only sell tickets because I wear short shorts... We'll f*** all of you 'cause not only am I a musician, I am the musician of the year... I love writing music and not only that, I can f***ing do it in a lime green bikini I love, with nail polish that I love to match, and I don't have to cover my body to be respected. I can wear whatever the f*** I want to wear and I'm still a musician". - Amy Taylor, Amyl and the Sniffers

"I grew up in a world that told girls they couldn't play rock 'n' roll". - Joan Jett.

This wasn't my experience, but the older I got the more I understood. Being told "I don't really like bands with girl singers," "you should wear a dress on stage" and "are you his girlfriend? Oh, are you in the band?" shows that whilst the world doesn't explicitly tell me that girls can't play rock 'n' roll, it still holds subconscious biases and expectations. One experience that I now laugh about is having a sound technician talk to my male band mate about the set up of my amps whilst I was standing next to him. Do these experiences affect me negatively? No. They give me the drive to go on stage, stare you down and shout in your face.

"Girls to the front" - Kathleen Hanna, Bikini Kill

The 1970s saw the likes of X-Ray Spex and The Slits paving the way, whilst the 1990s saw Bikini Kill's Kathleen Hanna shouting "girls to the front" at their gigs to encourage women to reclaim the space once dominated by moshing blokes. Bikini Kill were routinely heckled on stage, having chains thrown at them on occasion. Not okay. Kathleen wanted to create a safe space for women. My view? I'd encourage women to enter mosh pits with the blokes and have it large just like they do. Treat each other with respect. Regardless of your identity, if you're there to cause trouble, you know where the door is. This is EQUALITY.

Bikini Kill spent their career being labelled 'Riot Grrrl' as a genre, defined by lyrical themes such as domestic abuse, patriarchy and classism. Riot Grrrl became a subculture of political activism. Bikini Kill and those who followed exuded empowerment, and thank God they did. They've been described as "fiery" and "abrasive" with "radical feminist" lyrics. If they were men, would these adjectives have been used? I doubt it. If the band consisted mainly of men, would they have been labelled a 'punk' band rather than Riot Grrrl? I think so. There are two ways of looking at it. On the one hand Riot Grrrl created a well-overdue platform to address important issues. On the other hand, did it limit the level of integration and equality obtainable for women within the genre of punk rock and oi? Regardless, there is no question that Riot Grrrl paved the way for many, including me.

"They say women can't play guitar as well as men. I don't pay the guitar with my vagina, so what difference does it make?" - Brody Dalle.

I'm in a band called The Meffs. I play four chords. I shout about society. I sweat profusely. I drink shandy on stage. I play with the best drummer. He's a bloke and he's top quality. I'm not deluded; I can't quit my job. But I've made it. I've made it in many ways. Being labelled a punk band without the label of 'female-fronted' is an achievement in itself. Is it more challenging being a woman in the punk and rock scenes? Yes. Is it more challenging being any minority in music? Yes. BUT you can still smash it hard. I'm confident in myself as a woman and as a lesbian, but most importantly as a person.

One day I'll have a quote but for now "female-fronted is not a genre".

Lily

<u>War Paint</u>

Put on your lipstick and pretend everything's okay.
There's a reason it's called war paint, honey,
And you'll be needing yours today.
The bolder the shade, the braver you feel.
They'll never work out what those bright reds conceal.

Steph, 26

The rite of passage to be a woman

I became a mum at age 29, and whilst that didn't seem young at the time, it was long before my friends who strung out getting married and having children until much later. As the first person to end up being a parent in my peer group, I felt black sheepish.

During the pregnancy, I realised something was wrong when I handed the keys over for my old flat and moved in with my partner, just one night before we picked up keys for our new house. I probably should have walked then, as he spent most of the night shouting at me that I had been lazy and calling me every name under the sun. I remember lying awake that night, pondering what to do. I felt trapped- here is the father of my child, and it turns out he is rather psychopathic.

We moved in together the next day, and I felt each and every day a growing sense of ill ease. I had to find the right words to talk to him, the right way to be, to stop him from flying at me, dressing me down and threatening to kill me. I couldn't believe my situation, as just a few years before I had been doing domestic violence work with homeless adults and I felt that I would never be in that situation myself. I didn't realise then, what I know now, is that abusers often rely on getting you pregnant or married so you can't get out.

He seemed pretty perfect when I met him; we'd been friends for a while before we got together and he was always really charming to everyone. Flirtatious, but in a romantic French way, or so I thought. The progression of our relationship was slow; we took our time - we had both fancied each other but had not made a move. It seemed like the perfect love story, until it wasn't.

Just a few days after my son was born I heard his dad yelling and breathing fire from upstairs 'I can't do this'... and he stomped downstairs. He told me to go and see to my child otherwise he 'might hurt him'. This freaked me out and then I took over everything from then on.

A few months later, things started to get really bad, I sunk into such a depression I wasn't sure how to go on and I would picture myself driving into oncoming traffic, or drowning myself in the bath. The only thing I held on to was my son, and this kept me going.

My partner would claim I was crazy and that I needed help, so I went to see a therapist. The therapist turned to me and told me that he was abusing me, and that I needed to create safe boundaries.

What they didn't tell me is what would happen next.

I came home and started to create some more boundaries and be firm about the abuse I was receiving.

He wrapped his hands around my throat. I remember him shouting so close to my face I could see the whites of his eyes....and it was terrifying.

I couldn't help but think how could it happen to me?

The truth is, it can happen to anyone.

I left him, finally, under police escort on the 15th January 2010. I made it out like most people do: with just the clothes on my back, and not many at that.

It was a freezing, extremely cold and snowy night. The police took us to a friend's house I would never usually go to - one I hadn't seen for so long - as I had to find somewhere to escape to where he couldn't find me.

We sofa surfed, I didn't make it out with a mobile phone, and I made it out without money or a purse so couldn't call anyone. In that moment I have never felt more desolate or broken, or more alive.

In the weeks that followed the mood lifted and my freedom felt hard won. I felt like I had just escaped from jail. A few days later we secured an emergency flat, and moved in, again with nothing. It was strange arriving that day. It made me realise a roof and walls doesn't make a home, as I threw my Gillet on my son for him to sleep warm, whilst I laid in the December chill with just a t-shirt on: It was all I made it out with. I remember in those days feeling defeated but somehow something switched in me.

One of my friends once said to me, 'You're the most resilient person I know; if you can bounce back, you not only bounce back but you come back better.' I promised myself in that moment that I was not going to have my life destroyed by this man.

I trudged in the snow with my pushchair down to a children's centre and the library to do a job application and decided in that crazy moment to apply to do a Master's degree. I didn't have any A levels or a degree. But I knew if I had five years' experience, I might be able to scrape in. Scrape in I did and got a conditional offer of staying on if I passed my first year.

I made a resolve then to become a chief executive, even though I really had hardly any management experience. I remembered reading somewhere in a Harvard review that women don't apply because they don't have all the skills on a person spec, and made it my mission to start applying.

12 months later, I became a CEO. It seemed alien at the time and I faced imposter syndrome all the time, but as time elapsed even though I wasn't a confident or a conventional CEO, I was definitely a good one. I was always wracked with self-doubt, but I realised that doubt accompanies every big change in our lives, and that we must carry doubt as a companion rather than an obstacle.

That fear is a marker that tells us we are stretching beyond our wildest dreams, and that if we are not doing things that make us afraid from time to time, we are perhaps not trying hard enough.

My life since has been one long adventure: we live in a beautiful countryside area now, we live in peace, quiet and tranquility and all this life feels like a long time ago. I wanted to share my story, to give hope to others living under the weight of domestic violence that there is life beyond leaving, and that our goals can exceed anything we can ever imagine possible even for our own lives.

I went to school with a class who were mostly pregnant or in jail by the time they were eighteen, and whilst many have begun to come out the other side, coming from this background did not make me feel entitled to success. Whilst I have lived a challenging life as a single parent, every day I am thankful that we are safe, that we have the rest of our lives to live, and that it is better to be a good single parent with no relationship, then living in the most terrifying one relationship of my lifetime.

We underestimate our own power and voices as women, and when we find our voices, we can become wildly powerful beyond compare. I dedicate my life now to being a fierce advocate of women's rights, of helping others, and lifting people out of poverty. My working life now is spent helping young entrepreneurs, as well as training new CEO's, who are ordinary people like you and me, with an extraordinary passion for doing something good.

I think a key defining moment for me was realising that the identity of being a victim did not have to define my future. I changed the way I looked at things and learned to tell my empowering story of transformation so that others could get a sense of what is possible. We limit our own potential often by thinking or feeling that we are not enough.

The truth is, the only thing a CEO knows that you don't, is how to ask for help from others around them to do all the things they don't know how to do. Become excellent at asking for help from those around you, and watch how life will gravitate towards you and give you everything you want and need.

Anna

I used to be ME

I used to wear my hair down, wear floaty dresses and sit in the sunshine watching the day fade away.
I was carefree with all the time in the world.
I was whoever I wanted to be, whenever I felt like it.

I was a person with hopes and dreams and endless positivity.
A person with real goals, with real opinions – strong opinions! - about topics that matter.
I had fiery debates and interesting conversations with interesting people.

I travelled the world. I learned, I always felt inspired and I inspired others. I wanted to save the world.
I was creative and motivated. I studied, I helped people, I explored. I loved every single person I met.
And I grew.

I used to laugh a lot and cry less.

I was Fierce. Confident. Passionate. Bold. Sexy. Brave. Fun. Playful.
I WAS SO FREE...

I admire her, I adore her and I miss her. I miss the person I used to be.
She is just a hazy, dreamlike memory sitting in the sunshine without a care in the world...

Because I am a mum now and I can't figure out how to be both people.
And I'm shrinking.

But my little warrior is completely and whole heartedly, unapologetically herself.
And SHE is fierce
And SHE is so free...

Sara, 34

The seven ages of me

I shredded my past today.

Not all of it, of course – just the bit from 1991-1997. I'll get back to that: stick with me.

Shakespeare famously wrote about the 'Seven Ages of Man' – look it up – but I'm going to write about the 'Seven Ages of Me.

Stage One: I grew up surrounded by grandparents, living with one set until I was three. It was an unremarkable childhood. I was never allowed to play with the other children in the street; instead, I joined in by standing on the step that my grandfather fixed to the front fence, his way of making sure I wasn't entirely isolated. We then moved next door to my paternal grandparents; as my grandmother preferred my father's previous fiancée, there was always friction. Our house was cold, and my mother wasn't the cuddliest person in the world. My sister was born when I was six, I assumed the role of big sister and, as she so often tells me, her 'real mum.' We're still really close.

Stage Two: Looking back my value was always measured by my successes, although I don't recall being aware of that. I loved primary school, always in the top three in my class, and never happy if I didn't beat the other two, both boys. I was an embryonic feminist even then, determined to be the best. In Year 6, one of my teachers asked me if my parents were proud of me. I thought he was talking about my rather successful role in the school show, completely surprised when he corrected me, saying that I had passed my 11+; my parents had told everyone but me. My maternal grandmother, however, loved to boast about my academic prowess, telling everyone I had 'passed for the Tech.' I chose not to go to the Girls' High School, preferring to attend a mixed sex school; I was in top stream every year, with the benefit of a Grammar school education, useful when I got my first job, albeit not the one I had planned.

Stage Three: I met my husband when I was just 17. My teenage years had been traumatic. My maternal grandmother had moved in when I was 11, and by then I was pretty screwed up. Nana was A* at manipulating us into feeling permanently guilty, reducing us all eventually to emotional wrecks, my mother and I both being put on Valium. His family was laid back, open, welcoming. He was – like his mum – down to earth, logical, straightforward: my saviour. And I have yet to meet someone who didn't instantly fall in love with 'handsome Phil,' my lovely father-in-law. Engaged at 19; married at 21; still together 47 years later.

Stage Four: It took me a long time to become a mother; nature wouldn't play ball, and I had a lot of hospital visits to try to get to the root of the problem. We'd reached the point of discussing adoption when I went down with a bout of bronchitis. I was feeling dreadful when I went to see my gynaecologist. I hopped up on to the examining couch, he took a quick look at my nethers, and I'll never forget his words – "Well, I'm not God, but I'm pretty close and I am 99% certain that you are pregnant." Did I whoop? Did I cheer? Did I burst into tears? I fainted and fell off the couch, reviving to him saying, "I'm not bothered about you, but we're not losing this baby at this stage!" 19 months later, son number two; four years after that son number three. Nature's blockage was well and truly unplugged! I loved being a fulltime mum. That time was priceless to me.

Stage Five: When my youngest son was about three, my husband said to me that now was the time for me to pursue my unfulfilled dream of becoming a teacher. (What he really said was "You'll drive me mad if you have nothing to do once all the boys are at school, so get out there and do your degree!") Teaching was something I had wanted to do since I was old enough to line up my dolls – and sometimes my grandma - and teddies in front of my blackboard and read them story after story. My sister also joined my little classroom under the lilac tree and could read pretty proficiently by the time she started school. I had indeed found my true vocation.

I'd left school with just four O'levels, enough to become a Secretarial trainee at a local engineering company. I had a happy 12 years there, becoming the Managing Director's personal secretary at the age of 20, a week before I got married; had to be successful, hey? By the time I left, girls were being encouraged to train as engineers in a hitherto male dominated profession.

So: 1991. All three sons at school. Uni.

"Will you still come home at weekends, Mummy?" My youngest found it hard to understand, so was given a day off to come with me. It was a complete success, his first introduction to Mummy's new world. "What did you learn about?" asked his father. "Knickers!" was his response. We had studied a poem called 'Underwear.'

After the first day of lectures, I was about to give up. I had NO idea what 'The Enlightenment' was, and strange words floated past my brain without landing. I felt like Rita, but without the hairdressing. Eventually it started to make sense, and I formed a strong bond with other women born in 1952, like me.

With support from my husband, I found that I COULD write decent essays. The University had convenient Study weeks that coincided with half term holidays. Piece of cake, hey? Not really. Add to the mix the drive to be the perfect mother whilst still creating stunning essays. Exhaustion hit. My drive to succeed was always there bubbling away under the surface, whispering in my ear. It was hard to explain to anyone, and the guilt that I felt when I insisted – shouted – to my children that, no, they couldn't spend half term with their friends because I had booked them into the Uni's activity week, still comes back to haunt me in those sleepless nights when my conscience feels the need to drag up every bad thing I have done, perceived or real. I had a complete melt down in my third year, and all my insecurities and fear of failure, of not being 'top,' threatened to drag me down beyond resurrection. I got through it, with the help of my husband and my sister, who talked me down and convinced me that I'd get through this. I did.

I got a First-class degree; a Masters; a teaching degree. Successful, right??

Stage Six: Teacher, in a tough secondary school. Many challenges; fantastic camaraderie. Content to be 'just' a classroom teacher? What do you think?! My sons were at secondary school; the pressure to be 'everywoman' was off. So: Head of Department, Deputy Head of Year, Head of Year, leaving when academic success took precedence over the wellbeing of the children – ironic, hey? I took early "retirement." Note the parenthesis; I had four more, child centred, jobs.

So: Stage Seven: "What do you want your sons to be, Miss?" "Easy: happy and healthy." Add 'Independent" to that mix, and they are, scattered around the globe. My final stage: 'International Grandmother." Australia, the Netherlands, Brighton: my 'other' homes. It's a strangely conflicting feeling; I have been to places I never would have gone, visiting my Aussie and Dutch grandchildren. Equally, it breaks my heart that I cannot do 'normal' grandmother things, but I cherish our precious times together.

So… which part of my life did I shred? Stage 5: mature student, my transitional stage, being an example to my sons, better financially to help them forge their own future; fulfilled yet guilt ridden; focussed on me when I should have been focussed of them? A first class student but a second class mother? I don't think they ever thought that. I think they've forgiven me for my period of 'neglect.'

These days, I tinker a bit with writing poetry. I penned the following, which sums up how I feel now. I hope you like it.

I need four lives
Consecutive, simultaneous; I don't care.

I need four lives.
One ordinary, everyday,
Grounded in the UK
Coffee mornings, writing evenings
Old friends, extended family.

I need four lives
One away, upside down
Reached by air
Filled with sunshine,
Hot days, mosquito nights.

I need four lives.
One so close, if I were a crow.
Straight travelling, no passport needed.
Coach, train, car.
A stony beach, a trendy bar.

I need four lives,
One with windmills,
Tulips, cheese and clogs
Impenetrable syntax
High and lows on a flat landscape.

I need four lives.
All of them routine,
Normal, grandkids-messy.

I have one life
Shared around the world
Delivered on Skype.

I make the most
Thankful that I can.

Di, 68

Why don't you just have a baby?

When I think about my own womanhood, a key piece of what makes me, me, is my periods and endometriosis. I feel lucky to have felt mostly confident with my lot growing up (apart from the normal teenage worries here and there) but the one thing I have always struggled with is the daily, weekly and monthly reminders from my body. There's a reason I have nicknamed my womb 'womb of doom!'

The biggest part of this struggle has been the lack of information, guidance and support from the medical profession and society as a whole. The majority of women have a period each month, and yet we still don't talk openly about it. I find it completely outrageous that something so natural, and arguably vital for our species' survival, is still essentially a taboo subject. Up until 2016, a real sanitary towel had never been featured on a television advert for feminine hygiene products before, and it took a further year for a company to actually use realistic red liquid to illustrate blood, rather than the classic 'blue' liquid we're all used to (BBC News, 2017). Heaven forbid period blood should actually look like blood! Real sanitary towels rather than CGI ones? Look away ladies before they cause you too much shame and embarrassment!

When I was younger we got a few lessons in puberty and sex education. In my experience these lessons were rushed and basic. What's more, they separated boys and girls to teach us, which seemed to set the tone that puberty for both sexes was something we should be embarrassed about and keep private. A vivid memory I have from that first 'period' lesson is my female Head Teacher rolling her eyes to our group of girls because my male class teacher (who was responsible for bringing in sanitary products for the show and tell bit) had actually brought an incontinence pad rather than a sanitary towel. He couldn't tell the difference, despite living with his wife and having a daughter himself. These were the first societal cues we were given about periods and how they should be viewed: embarrassing, confusing and don't talk to the boys about them!

Don't get me wrong, in my teens I talked to my mum and my friends about my periods, but it's hard to understand what is normal when everyone's experience is unique. I remember being wildly jealous when I found out some of my friends had 3 day long periods, with little pain, and one even stopped bleeding whenever she lay down! I decided then to stop having the conversation as no one seemed to understand how hard I found it. The two week minimum bleeding, physically exhausted and always concerned that I'd bled through and stained my clothes. The panic that I hadn't brought enough sanitary towels to school to see me through. I used to faint and be crippled over on the floor barely able to move from the pain. I had to set alarms at night to get up and change my sanitary towel because it would overflow otherwise, and I became so distraught about staining everything I used to only sit on an old towel on the sofa just in case. It was exhausting, and it happened every month without fail. Looking back, I am thankful that our family could afford to supply me with the amount of sanitary products I needed, I know some girls and women are not so lucky.

My first visit to the doctors about my periods at around 15 resulted in the classic quick fix I'm confident most women of my age have experienced: they put me straight on the pill. I was in and out of the consulting room in 10 minutes, had barely been listened too, and the response I got was 'it's normal, you'll have to put up with it'. I was given no support, no further guidance on what I was experiencing and just a quick fix using contraception. Needless to say, it didn't 'fix' the issue, but for years to come my repeated visits to the doctor meant an endless parade through the encyclopaedia of contraception. The doctors, and even myself by that time, had forgotten what I'd originally asked for help with.

I continued on, hating each month dealing with the pain, the bloating and inflammation of my stomach. Struggling to sleep, concentrate, or to feel good dependent on what date of the month it was. Spending hundreds of pounds on sanitary towels, tampons and iron supplements and feeling angry that I had to pay (and pay tax!) for something to help me function in society while my body did something so natural.

It was much later, when I started having to take time off work due to my periods, that I decided to try again at the doctors. Luckily by that point I had an incredibly supportive partner who empowered me to understand that what I experienced wasn't something I just had to put up with.

And this is when it happened. I was in my mid 20's, clearly struggling, and after listening to my explanations the doctor asked me if I wanted to have children. I was stunned by the question at first. Despite the obvious association I couldn't understand why this was being brought up. I replied, haltingly, that yes I did, but not right now. My doctor visibly relaxed and said 'well it will all get better once you have a baby, so why don't you think about it'. It was only after discussing this afterwards with others that I felt the outrage. Yet again I had been brushed off, given no information, help or guidance and now I'd simply been told to have a baby to solve my problems! What if I decided I didn't want to have children? Did that mean I had to live my life in pain and agony because that was the best modern science had to offer?! I've since learnt that (A) I'm not alone in receiving this 'advice;' (B) it usually doesn't help anyway ; and (C) it can actually be challenging for women with endometriosis to conceive in the first place.

It took another 2 years for me to be officially 'diagnosed' with endometriosis. By this point I'd been trying to get help for 12 years. Despite this being a disease that affects an estimated 176 million women worldwide (Endometriosis.org, 2021) there is still a severe lack of support and education via medicine, even for those who have been diagnosed. What I find so disappointing is that we haven't moved on; our society with all our incredible advancements in other areas are still shockingly slow and behind the times when it comes to women's medicine.

The previous year has been a hard one, but thankfully we're seeing some positive change as we move into 2021 with the 'tampon tax' being abolished as of 1 January 2021 (Gov.uk, 2021).

This will help tackle issues such as period poverty in the future but hopefully will start better conversations and education to avoid embarrassment. I'm massively thankful to the businesses and charities helping educate and improve awareness about periods and endometriosis. I hope that this continues to encourage open conversation and begin normalising periods in everyday life, from a young age.

Period rant, over!

Imogen, 29

The Break-Up

There's something special about a strong female friendship. The sisterhood. As a woman, your female friends are your biggest cheerleaders and your fiercest advocates, they listen without judgement, are your greatest advisors and your strongest supporters; they are sad for your sadness and happy for your happiness. People say that behind every great man is an even greater woman, but behind every great woman is a gang of other great women bigging her up.

I've never had one "BFF", but I do have a handful of besties who I love fiercely and who I sincerely hope will be in my life until we are old and grey and spending our retirement day drinking and gossiping on a Wednesday just because we can. But I'm pragmatic too; I'm an advocate of the old adage that people come into your life for a reason, a season or a lifetime. Not every friendship will last forever; people change throughout their lives and their relationships ebb and flow with them. But what are you supposed to do when a best friend who you thought was there for a lifetime decides to dump you out of the blue?

I know so many women who have been through a friendship break up, and most of them say they are still not over it, long after past romantic relationships have been forgotten. A friendship breakup with a platonic friend can be just as traumatic and leave just as big a hole in your life as the loss of a romantic partner, but the former isn't given the same level of credence. Taylor Swift doesn't write songs about lost friends. They don't make films about moving on from being dumped by your bestie. As a society, we don't allow ourselves the emotional space to grieve for a lost friendship in the same way that we do a lost lover. For me, the biggest shock was just how much it hurt.

If a lover decides that they want to end your relationship, they owe you an explanation. A ten year romance doesn't just end without some sort of discussion being had about it. There is a whole myriad of admin that comes with a romantic break up. By the end of it you at least know where you stand. With friendships, however, the rules aren't the same; a friend can just cut you out with no warning, and you're just left feeling heartbroken and wondering what you did wrong.

I can pinpoint when she decided she didn't want to be friends with me anymore but I can't pinpoint why - and believe me I have replayed every conversation from that time over and over in my head to work out whether it was something I said or did, but I'm as certain as I can possibly be that nothing out of the ordinary happened. Whatever triggered it, she suddenly emotionally checked out of our friendship, and what followed was months of her reluctantly attending events that were already planned, rarely responding to my attempts at contact and making excuses every time I asked to see her, until finally there was no reason to see or speak to each other.

Her disinterest in me during that time was painful. Mutual friends tried to remain impartial to start with but slowly our group drifted apart in favour of her. There were little digs on social media obviously aimed at me. I asked her directly what was wrong several times and she always brushed me off by saying she was "just busy." In hindsight, I don't know why I put up with it for so long - in actual fact I didn't only put up with it, I actively and desperately tried to rekindle something that wasn't there.

Obviously there was a reason she felt the need to do what she did. Adults generally don't go from being best friends with someone one week to almost completely indifferent to them the next without good reason. I'm not arrogant enough to think that I'm not partially to blame for our friendship ending.

Furthermore, I don't judge her for wanting to end it - if I had irreparably offended or upset her, or I wasn't being a good friend in some way, or even if our friendship had simply run its course for her and she didn't need or want me in her life anymore – whatever her reason, it was absolutely her prerogative to do so. But I do judge her for the way she did it. It was brutal. Way more brutal than a confrontation would have been.

Rejection without an explanation is so hard to process. For the friend doing the dumping it may feel like the easier and kinder thing to do to just leave the friendship rather than face the difficult conversation, but it's absolutely, categorically not; in fact, it's cruel. When you've been in any kind of relationship with someone for a long time, be it platonic or otherwise, if you want to leave that relationship then that person deserves an explanation. I've been the friend doing the dumping before and I made sure that my now-ex friend knew exactly why I would no longer be continuing our friendship. Was that a tough conversation to have? Yes- but I can sleep soundly knowing that she's not torturing herself wondering what she did wrong or why I am no longer in her life, and it meant I got a clean break too. Closure is important. It allows us to recover and move on.

It surprised me to learn how many of my other girlfriends had been through something similar when I spoke to them about what had happened to me. Some things became abundantly clear through those conversations: that everyone who had been on the receiving end of being unexpectedly cut out had not recovered from the emotional toll of it, and that none of them had ever really talked about it. It's weird that it should feel like such a taboo subject; are we subconsciously scared that by telling other friends what happened it might make them suddenly realise that there's something wrong with us and leave us too?

I try not to let what happened with her affect my other friendships, but if a friend doesn't message me back or cancels plans there's always that fleeting thought that maybe they don't want to be my friend anymore and I start anxiously wondering if I've done something wrong. I second guess my own behaviour. It feels ridiculous to admit this at 33 years old but our experiences shape us and here I am.

I'm not naive enough to think that one day she might make contact to give me the explanation I've craved for so long. It's been years now; my anger has faded and my sadness doesn't smart like it used to. I've moved on, made new friends who I have more in common with, and I've realised that maybe she and I weren't as suited as I once thought.

I never got closure, but sharing this has been cathartic and maybe that's as close to closure as I need.

I'm happy now, and I hope she's happy too.

Josie, 33

From me to me

Preparedness,
I wish I had prepared less.
Over-thinking,
What was I thinking?
Abundance of perspective, seemingly possible,
Accept impossible.
Hard is fine, good is fine, fine is fine;
Mine, always. Mind control.
Can't go further, but you will have more.
Befriend unsure.
Wishing time away, never.
It never returns.
Comparison kills, love fills.
Superficial surface strangers,
Pause, cry, let it go; lean on those that know.
Negativity breeds,
Possibility and positivity succeeds.
Where are we going? It will be better then, when...
Pause, just live the moment.
Getting this done, rushing, that done,
Stop.
Look what we've done.
Always stop.
Look what we've done.
Admire their perfection.

Elle, 31

"YOU HAVE CANCER"

Sorry, what now? Are you talking to me? Nah, you can't be. I am only 35. I am really fit and healthy. Ok, maybe I eat a bit more chocolate than I probably should and I may opt for a glass of wine in place of a peppermint tea at the weekend, but you can't be talking to me. Please? Please don't be talking to me.

Unfortunately, they were talking to me. There I was, at the age of 35 being told I had ovarian cancer.

A million thoughts instantly filled my head.

Was this it? Was this the way I was going to see out my days? I would now be a cancer patient and that sounds weird. I would have to explain to my family and friends. I would have to sort out my job. I have so much work on at the moment – who will get stuck with that? Would I be able to work anymore? Could I sustain paying my mortgage and bills? Would my husband have to alter his life and would we need to live elsewhere? How would my friends cope? My poor parents and siblings. My grandparents. What about chemo? Am I going to lose my hair? What will my step-daughter think? Will I be an embarrassment?

This is the thing about womanhood. There is this intuitive, intrinsic part of you that juggles not only your life, your thoughts and feelings, but carries the weight of the world's thoughts and feelings too. I don't know how you learn to do this, but it is inherently part of your make-up. A blessing and a curse.

In those first moments of sheer 'I have cancer' panic, few of my thoughts were solely about myself. On reflection, the impact and power of this is tremendous. To me, I now know this is a superpower. Often an unconscious superpower.

The superpower that is womanhood.

Now before I go on, I feel compelled to tell you that I am one of the lucky ones. I had a very rare cancer and I was so very fortunate enough to get early diagnosis. Owing to this (and a pretty amazing surgical team), I am cancer free and I even got to a position where I did not have to embark on the chemotherapy treatment that was originally planned for me. This is not a sad story and I am incredibly lucky.

I am now nearly 3 years post diagnosis and although I am two major surgeries later and now menopausal due to having a hysterectomy and I am sporting a scar that runs from my belly button, well about as far down as you can go... I am wonderfully, beautifully and blissfully cancer free.

In retrospect, the journey that I have been on is an absolute insult to womanhood. I have never been the bearer of a child and that choice is not one I now have. I had a 'women's cancer' – does that make me less of a woman? My reproductive organs were faulty.

As I mentioned, the earliest of plans for me was that I was going to be having some chemotherapy. Interestingly, I had some, what I imagine are common and understandable, thoughts about this prospect. These thoughts through time, recovery and lots of reflection have been transformed into one of the most valuable and powerful messages of womanhood that I have ever experienced.

Despite my superpower of carrying everybody else's thoughts with my own, one of the thoughts I did have, and I remember saying out loud, was, "I am going to lose my hair, my eyebrows, my eyelashes and maybe my nails. All of the things that make me feel feminine. All of the things that make me feel beautiful."

This was a real blow to me. My life was about to change forever. My appearance is what I see when I look in the mirror or the reflection that stares back at me as a walk past a window. It is what I see when a friend takes a photograph of me and shares it on social media. It is what my friends, family and colleagues see. It is something that is there.

Always. All of the time. We all have an appearance. This is a whole topic in its own right. We all have different thoughts, feelings and dependencies on our appearances and this can have an incredible impact on wellbeing.

I sat in my room and looked at my drawer of hair products. Hair spray, hair masks, hair serum, hairbrushes, straighteners, hair dryers. What would I do with all of this stuff? Would I ever need it again?

This is where my story became interesting. Something switched. And to this day, I think, no, I know, that this is due to the superpower of womanhood.

Somehow, some way, I had this ability to turn these feelings of complete loss and horror around. My perception shifted. Losing my hair, eyebrows, lashes or nails was not defining me. This was not going to be a loss. This was going to be an empowering and pivotal point in my life. This was an opportunity. An opportunity to live, thrive and survive. How many people are there who would do anything to have the opportunity to have chemotherapy, lose their hair and be given a chance?

All of a sudden I knew. Womanhood, being beautiful, feeling beautiful, was not about hair, or nails or the way people look at you, or even the way you may look at yourself. It is your soul, your being, your words, your empathy, your kindness, your love. Womanhood: your superpower.

This is badass. This is womanhood. With this, you can do anything and go anywhere.

This takes me back to a moment when my mother (who is also now doing well) had chemotherapy for her cancer in 2013. I remember shopping for her and calling her to ask her if she needed any toiletries like shower gel, shampoo. Oh no, I just said shampoo – she had just lost her hair. We both fell silent...

Then, I added – unless you would prefer some furniture polish and a duster? At this, we laughed, uncontrollably.

This is a perfect example of my mother using her superpower of womanhood. In her worst and most personal moments of vulnerability, she was able to adapt and use this as a moment to thrive and drive forwards with complete ownership and decorum.

I was able to use my hurt, worry, upset and clumsy dialogue to turn this into humour to get us through what was such a painful time. This conversation diffused so much for us and helped us get her through her cancer journey.

We are stronger, fiercer and more incredible than we give ourselves credit for. We have this inherent ability to just survive. With grace, beauty, love and light. And this is all done whilst juggling not only our emotions and life but carrying and supporting those around us.

When you feel alone, stressed, scared - which at times you will - look in the mirror and recognise all that you are. When you aren't able to do that, ask another woman because she will hold you up, look you in the eyes and tell you. You are exactly as you are meant to be. That is womanhood.

Sara, 38

A lockdown baby

To all the Mothers who raised a baby during lockdown, you are not alone and you did an amazing job during an unthinkable time…

I was sat on the toilet thinking about what I was going to wear to my friend's baby shower when it happened. My first baby was four weeks early so I shouldn't have been surprised that this one was coming 10 days early, but when my waters broke, just for a moment I thought, "This is too soon." I shouted down to my husband that I needed help and to grab my phone.

I did what you are told to do and rang triage to tell them my waters had broken. They then asked the usual questions: are you sure? When did it happen? Do you have any pain? Since this was my second baby, I knew it was definitely my waters and that my contractions would start a little later (as this is what happened last time). Anyway, while on the phone the midwife asked me:

"Have you been abroad recently?"
"No"
"Have you been in contact with anyone who has recently returned from China, Spain or Italy"
"No"
"Alright you can come in"

At that moment I knew what the questions were about, but I still thought it was a little odd. I went in to hospital as instructed and four hours later I had a baby boy. I was discharged that evening and I went home to enjoy being a mum to two boys.

Fast forward three weeks and the unimaginable happened - the whole of the UK went into lockdown! At the time it was all a bit strange because I was still on that high you have after having a baby. I was trying to juggle a toddler and a new-born, all the while trying to master breastfeeding again.

As the weeks went by, however, the severity of lockdown started to hit me. Only a handful of people had the pleasure of meeting my new baby and because of lockdown no one else could. This would mean family and friends would miss out on those precious baby cuddles and I couldn't get the additional help every Mother needs after a new baby. The more time that passed the more I felt isolated, trapped and the four walls that made up my living room became a sight I hated.

My baby only had me and therefore became very clingy. He spent 24 hours a day, 7 days a week glued to me and my boobs. On the plus side we mastered breastfeeding quite quickly and he gained weight daily. Unfortunately, though, he never learnt the art of patience - with nowhere to go I could easily feed on demand. He didn't have to wait because we were out somewhere and I couldn't sit down, or wait because we were in the car on the way somewhere. He would just cry and root then I would feed him.

As I look back on what happened and the situation, I found myself in I am so glad this was my second child. I can't imagine going through all the anxieties of lockdown on top of the anxieties that come with being a first-time parent. There have been no baby groups to lean on other mothers for advice and support or to celebrate baby milestone's with; no health visitor drop-in sessions to check my baby was gaining enough weight and talk to a professional; and no breastfeeding groups to support you with the struggles of breastfeeding.

They say it takes a village to raise a baby but apart from my husband there has been nobody: the village was closed due to lockdown.

Another thing I find interesting is the noticeably different personalities between my two boys. I know all children are different but there are some differences between them that I expect may have something to do with the challenges of lockdown:

- Baby two has no patience; if he wants something he then expects it to be immediately given to him.

- He also until recently hated going in the car. The second we put him in the car seat he would scream until we reached our destination. Thank God he has grown out of that one!
- He cries when someone unfamiliar comes into the house. He's just not used to this and he is clearly anxious.
- He doesn't like anyone new approaching him in public. Even an unthreatening sweet old lady who stops to say 'what a lovely little boy' can make his lip quiver and start him off crying.
- He hates crowded places, not that we have been to many due to lockdown 2 & 3. But when we have been into the town centre on a busy day or if the supermarket is full, he gets very agitated, his eyes dart around the place as if he's looking out for danger and sometimes we have to just hold him tight to comfort him.

As time passes and he is exposed to more people I hope he will move past these issues but I can't help but wonder if this will have a longer-term effect on him. My first born is extremely sociable and loves seeing people. He loves to talk to everyone and gets very excited to go in the car or experience new places. He is not bothered by crowd places and likes to be independent (sometimes a little too much). As a mother, of course I want the best for my children and I know confidence in life is invaluable.

However, one positive I will always take from this situation and experience is the amount of time we got to spend together as a family of four. When our baby was born my husband had his usual two weeks paternity leave then returned to work. Less than a month later we all went into lockdown and he was furloughed; that then meant he got to spend weeks at home. I will always be thankful for that time as a family.

Lockdown has of course been difficult for everyone in some aspect; no matter what your situation or background is there have been challenges to face.

However, as a woman and a mother I have not only experienced the pain and heartbreak of missing my family and friends but also the constant worry and stress of concern for my children's welfare and I think so many women can relate to this. Mother or not, women are often self-appointed care givers, often guilty of putting others before themselves. When it comes to our children this is no exception.

Looking after not only myself but also two children through this incredibly challenging period of history has really shown me how resilient and tough women can be. I can only hope that as we ease back into normal life my children prove to be just as resilient.

Rebecca, 32

Changed

The smell of antiseptic repulsed her. How could something so invasive smell so impersonal? She sat watching the big hand circulate the clock facing her, just like she had focused on the clock which taunted her during every after- school detention. Anything to take her away from her surroundings. Focus: tick tock, tick tock.

She thought back to her first secondary school boyfriend and to how he often forgot to take his iron supplement that he insisted was crucial to treat his self-proclaimed ME. She wondered how if he forgot that pill...just once (maybe twice), how he would feel to be left with a whole other life to claim? He would have been more careful of course. How careless she was. How selfish.

Her eyes darted back to the clock in nervous anticipation. Only minutes had passed. The weight of her decision bore over her as she shuffled in her seat, and the regret of declining the offer of company washed over her as a single tear fell.

As if in an outer body, she moved towards the door, visions of Sunday mornings in bed with her sweet-smelling newborn tucked between silk sheets pulling her towards the exit sign. Sanity prevailed as she reclaimed her seat. She didn't want this and what could be worse than bringing an unloved soul alone into this world... This?

No amount of regret or will could transport her mind somewhere else. She was there. Drowning in the injustice of it all, thoughts of him sinking pints oblivious to the decisions she faced. No regret or will could take turn back time. Only a doctor's precision and strong drugs could do that.

3 hours. 3 hours passed by as I waited for her impatiently, aware of my own ridiculousness for even entertaining my own boredom as an inconvenience. 3 hours and the door finally opened and there she was. Tired. Broken. I took her shaking hand in mine as we silently walked back to the car. I was her rock in a sea of undeserved self-loathing and grief. 'It will be ok' I say as I hold her hand tightly, the hand of a different woman from the girl I had known for so long.

Anonymous.

Me, My Mother, Death and Life

In 1990, when I was 26, my mother died from cancer. In various ways, her death stopped the clock for me. I was not an emotionally mature 26; I was still my mother's child, needing her help to get through her death, just when it was all she could do to get through it herself. In the early years afterwards, when I thought of her, it was from the vantage point of her child, because that was how we left things.

Strange things happen in grief and over this same period and since, I developed a bit of a fixation with the number 57, my mother's age at her death. My internal antenna assumed a state of constant alert for passing inconsequential mentions on TV and radio. Unremarkable events became noteworthy and personal. Then last year I turned 57 myself, and I realised, all this time I have been counting, in anticipation of my own arrival at this point: the year I might reach my mother again, maybe even for the first time properly. It is an odd thing though, to catch one's parent up; it shouldn't really be possible. My mother was, and should always remain, 31 years older than me. Yet here I am.

My mother did not have a good death, by which I mean, much sadness and loss led up to it. In the two years previously, she lost her marriage and her home of 30 years. She suffered these losses very deeply. She believed, and it was hard at the time not to feel this also, that the cancer that would eventually kill her grew quite literally out of these events.

Over this time, small notes appeared on the kitchen walls; notes to self: 'Expect nothing. Live frugally on surprise'. She began to write a diary, which I still have. I read it, once only, in the months after her death. Somewhere also there is an old cassette tape, a recording of a visit she made to a clairvoyant at an especially desperate point. I remember my anger at that woman, who claimed to offer my mother hope, and took extra money from her for a recording of her anguish. These things - a diary, a tape – terrible as they are, we can't destroy, for they are filled with her, for better or for worse.

Mostly, my mother didn't want to speak about what was happening to her. But once, in a rare conversation about the fact of her death, she promised to contact me afterwards, if she could. This profound moment, which sounds trite written down, was unwise in retrospect, giving rise rather predictably to a second preoccupation over the following months and years: how to interpret my mother's silence. For it did not result in a mature acceptance of the finality of her death, but instead in multiplying insecurities about other possible explanations, most of which did not reflect well on me.

My mother did come to me intermittently, in dreams, but these were rarely the happy reunions I wished for. In one, I opened the door of a rarely used downstairs room in our old family home and found her - a mannequin - lying broken in a pile of bits on the floor; her face looking up at me, her real face, imploring me to help. Instead, in that moment, I could only retreat as fast as I could, and shut the door on that awful apparition. Then, once the door was shut, I couldn't open it again, for fear of seeing not just desperation in my mother's face, but disappointment now too. Disappointment in me.

I have gone back and back to that door and lived with what lies behind it. What actually lies behind it, I know, is a theme of neglect that has pursued me – my knowledge that I could have done more for my mother. Then I wanted her to be stronger (the kind of 'strong' I suppose that my father might have stayed with). Now I see that she wasn't weak; she was simply reeling in the most human way from a series of cataclysmic losses, the most recent, the impending loss of her own life. But these were our losses too, my sister, my brother and I; we were all reeling.

------- ~ -------

I didn't go on to have my own children, although I've thought a great deal about motherhood and wondered how that rite of passage might have impacted upon my understanding of my mother.

For whatever else qualifies us as 'woman', and I don't of course mean to say that childbirth is a prerequisite, one can no longer exclusively be a child when one gives birth to a child of one's own.

Now, at 57, and many other milestones further on, the times and context I live in are so far removed from hers, but still, I imagine it, me and my mother face to face as women, and for fleeting lovely moments I can actually grasp it. More importantly, I have the equilibrium in myself to find pleasure from this safe distance in reflecting back on her life.

When she married a farmer, my mother married an all-consuming way of life, which was, on the face of it, a bit of a misfit. Her interests were more in the arts. She was bookish, she loved words; she was a natural researcher, a born academic really, but without the opportunity to pursue that career beyond university, as her father's death redirected her into employment, and then marriage added a further full-stop. She was passionate about genealogy, a hobby which back then meant holidays scraping moss off gravestones, and hours poring over library microfiches. How the Internet would have changed things for her! But in 1990 she had only just acquired her first Word Processor (an occasion I remember as tremendously exciting.)

In her younger years, she loved dancing. Dancing in fact brought my parents together, but ironically marriage really ended it for them. Or farming did at least. Music remained with her though; she sang Madrigals, loved opera, adored Wagner. She filled with colour, warmth and light what might otherwise have been a dark old farmhouse, with its long corridors. Instead, our home abounded with beautiful and interesting things; often rescued and restored. In my sister and me, my mother instilled a love of art, antique fairs and bric-a-brac, of collecting china and bringing old bits of furniture back to life.

My mother always wrote in blue ink with her maroon fountain pen, and generous, forward-flowing handwriting. She wrote copious lists, themselves testimony to a life of service to a family, as a mother, wife, homemaker.

Her lists, on bits of card, still bookmark her annotated cookery books, transporting me back to the familiar recipes of my childhood.

With the exception of my father's office, every room in our rambling farmhouse was invested with my mother's hand. But her room, and the thoroughfare for the rest of the house, was the kitchen. When she married, she didn't cook, but this was an expectation of her role and she set herself to it, becoming an exceptional one. There is a picture of her, apron on, leaning over the sink, mixer in hand, and if I say this is how I remember her best, I don't mean it badly. There was always life and I was never lonely if I was in the kitchen with my mother cooking. But nonetheless I wonder how she felt about the relentless duty to put food on the table. She did it without complaint, but without much thanks either. There must have been days she missed, but I can't remember them.

It seems to be a peculiarly female thing: to sacrifice, in the service of others, versions of themselves they might have been. Maybe more so for my mother's generation, but still true, I think. Of course, we can say, we have all chosen paths or been channelled along them, and in doing so closed doors on others. And I could also say that my parents were partners, running a farm together. But still, my father was the farmer, my mother the farmer's wife.

My mother would be 88 this year, this complex, interesting, loyal woman, who gave and gave of herself. At 57, she didn't want to die, but neither then could she see a purpose in living beyond her marriage and the farm. That bleak fog would have lifted though, and new versions of herself would have been waiting. She would have studied, she would have worked, there would have been new projects, maybe a late career. Or maybe she would have travelled instead. There would have been rich new friendships. She would have loved again. And she would have been loved.

For mum.

Rowena, 57

About the Author

Alex Freeman grew up in the UK's oldest record town of Colchester. She is one of two daughters to her Mother who she largely credits for her love of reading and of books. Now a Mother of two of herself her interests include reading, crafting and poetry. A passionate advocate for women's rights, Alex has made it her personal mission to empower women to share their stories.

Printed in Great Britain
by Amazon